Inspiration, Not Replication

*How Teachers Are Leading
School Change From the Inside*

Edited by
Stephen F. Hamilton
Randy Scherer

HIGH TECH HIGH

Inspiration, Not Replication:
How Teachers are Leading School Change from the Inside

Copyright © 2017 by High Tech High

This work was made possible by the California Career Pathways Trust and the California Department of Education

Publisher: Randy Scherer
Editors: Stephen Hamilton and Randy Scherer

Featuring research and writing by High Tech High educators: Mike Amarillas, Lillian Hsu, Kali Frederick, Stephanie Lytle, and Daisy Sharrock

Published by High Tech High
Distributed by High Tech High and the High Tech High Graduate School of Education

High Tech High
2861 Womble Road
San Diego, CA 92106

High Tech High Graduate School of Education
2150 Cushing Road
San Diego, CA 92106

www.hightechhigh.org
gse.hightechhigh.org

Inspiration, Not Replication

How Teachers Are Leading
School Change From the Inside

Edited by
Stephen F. Hamilton
Randy Scherer

Table of Contents

Ashanti Branch, PBL Leadership Academy Guest Faculty, works with Al Zadeh, a math teacher at Warren High School.

Preface

Randy Scherer
California Career Pathways Trust
PBL Leadership Academy

In the spring of 2015, the California Department of Education's California Career Pathways Trust (CCPT) partnered with High Tech High Schools (HTH) to develop and implement a new professional education program for teams of educators from schools, districts, and counties across the state of California that had won CCPT grants.

Beginning in 2014, CCPT grants were awarded in two rounds over two years to support the development of educational programs designed to facilitate student access to high-skill and high-wage jobs in growing or emerging sectors of local and regional economies. CCPT grantees implemented or expanded a wide range of programs: internships, externships, and related work-based learning efforts; professional development for educators; and work to develop project-based learning methodologies in a variety of contexts. The CCPT community recognized that project-based learning holds the potential to achieve many of the goals of career technical education and of traditionally "academic" classes, by offering educational experiences that are rich in academic content and skills, connections to communities beyond school, and opportunities to enter postsecondary education and employment.

Broadly speaking, project-based learning is an educational approach that engages educators and students in authentic work that is grounded in real-world contexts, and demands real-world solutions. Work of this nature necessarily continues for an extended period of time—a class may spend weeks, months, or even years pursuing a single complex, challenging question. Students and teachers address questions such as "Why is there gun violence in our community and what should we do about it?" or "How can we teach others about what lives in our environment?" To answer these questions students may work in one class or many, and they can acquire broad and deep content knowledge and myriad skills at essentially any age level (or even in multi-age groups). For example, kindergartners, middle schoolers, or high school students may teach others what lives in the environment near their school by creating field guides of the local flora and fauna with their scientific drawings of plants and animals, along with their descriptions of what they discover—just as wildlife biologists do. In project-based learning, students do not simply learn about a subject, they become someone: students making a field guide are not just learning about the environment, they become environmental scientists and journalists, and the rigor of their work is measured according to how closely they adhere to adult or professional standards in the field.

At HTH, project-based learning is used as a methodology to achieve equity in the classroom. Because projects have multiple entry points for students and demand varying skills and knowledge, a diverse cohort of students can engage in shared work. Their differences in past academic histories and personal interests do not stop them from working together in the same classroom; diversity is an advantage, as students contribute new perspectives, bring new skills, and open new avenues for learning.

HTH was developed by a coalition of educational, civic, and business leaders in San Diego, and opened as a single high school in September 2000 with plans to serve approximately 450 students and act as an incubator for best practices in education. HTH is guided by four connected design principles—equity, personalization, authentic work, and collaborative design—that set aspirational goals and create the foundation for HTH's approach to teaching and learning. HTH has evolved into an integrated network that includes 13 schools on three campuses serving more than 5,000 students in grades K–12, and an adult-learning environment that includes a Teacher Credentialing Program, and the High Tech High Graduate School of Education, which offers masters' degree and professional development programs serving educators from the region, the nation, and around the world.

The PBL Leadership Academy brought together several elements of HTH-facilitated professional development:

- PBL Leadership Academy participants worked through one school year in small teams dedicated to addressing authentic needs in their local context through a leadership project.
- Participants attended multi-day Leadership Institutes at the HTH Forum and in HTH schools in the fall and spring. The Leadership Institutes featured interactive workshops led by HTH staff and students, and nationally-known guest faculty.
- Each PBL Leadership Academy team was supported by a Team Mentor, who is a practicing HTH teacher, and an expert in their subject matter and in project-based learning.
- Team Mentors made multi-day visits to their teams' schools to facilitate a variety of professional

development activities. Some hosted large events featuring workshops in PBL practices for teachers from across a school, district, or even a county, while others led smaller sessions focused on supporting the specific projects of their team. Team members and their mentors co-designed the visits.

- The PBL Leadership Academy staff curated a variety of online resources, and participant teams met with their HTH Team Mentor regularly online for planning sessions, critiques, and project reflections.

The work of the educators who participated in the PBL Leadership Academy, and in broader CCPT efforts, is presented in two publications: *Inspiration, Not Replication: How Teachers Are Leading School Change From the Inside* and the accompanying volume *Hands and Minds: A Guide to Project-Based Learning for Teachers by Teachers*. The first captures stories of educators who embarked on journeys of transformation, of their classrooms, schools, and themselves; the second is a guide to the methodologies of project-based learning.

These books were created by HTH educators—their research comes from their classrooms, their schools, their experiences as mentors to educators in the PBL Leadership Academy, site visits to PBL Leadership Academy schools across California, and interviews with nationally known experts and the teachers and students in these books (student names contained in these publications are pseudonyms).

The two volumes, *Inspiration, Not Replication* and *Hands and Minds* are complementary, and may be read separately or together in any order. Just as the work of the hand cannot be separated from that of the mind, the methods that educators and students use in project-based learning cannot be separated from their personal stories. We hope that many educators, students, and families will see themselves and their own schools in these pages, and that they will be inspired and aided in continuing to create and recreate those schools.

References and Resources

1   "California Career Pathways Trust (CCPT)" California Department of Education, December, 2016, www.cde.ca.gov/ci/ct/pt/

2   "About Us" High Tech High Schools, August 2016, www.hightechhigh.org/about-us/

Educators participate in a design thinking workshop at the PBL Leadership Academy.

Inspiration, Not Replication

Introduction

Stephen F. Hamilton
Professor Emeritus
High Tech High Graduate School of Education

S chools are notoriously resistant to change. Two decades ago Richard Elmore wondered, "...why, when schools seem to be constantly changing, teaching practice changes so little, and on so small a scale."[1] Elmore's question highlights three issues in the problem of change. One is the appearance of change that proves unreal. As Seymour Sarason put it in *The Culture of the School and the Problem of Change*, "The more things change, the more they stay the same."[2] The second issue is the difficulty of changing actual teaching. Schedules change, class sizes change, new technologies are introduced, but teachers tend to teach the way they were taught. Third, when promising practices emerge, even after their effectiveness has been demonstrated, they usually fail to spread beyond a few islands of excellence. Making substantive changes to improve teaching—and learning—on a large scale remains a daunting challenge for educators. Much depends upon our success. The best hope our society has of promoting prosperity and reducing inequity is to raise the quality of education for all our citizens. Failing to master this challenge threatens our economic prosperity and political stability.

The stories in this book are a partial response to this challenge. They are about teachers, administrators, and support specialists working diligently, intelligently, and creatively to bring project-based learning (PBL) into their schools, a set of principles and practices that have demonstrated how all students can acquire both the kind of knowledge and skills addressed by conventional instruction and tests, and "deeper learning" too, including problem solving, collaboration, and communication, competencies that are essential to success in employment, civic engagement, and lifelong learning.[3] While the companion volume to this text, *Hands & Minds: A Guide to Project-Based Learning for Teachers by Teachers*, is about creating PBL curricula, this one is about how PBL is introduced to schools and how teachers make the change from more conventional pedagogy.

Adoption of PBL in these schools occurred in the context of the California Career Pathways Trust, established by the state legislature to support the implementation of the "Career Pathways" approach, which encourages educators to partner with employers, both to help design curricula and instruction to assure that graduates are prepared to be productive workers, and to gain access to learning opportunities in the workplace. As the name implies, having a Career Pathway orients a student to a future goal and ideally is accompanied by career education and counseling that begins well before high school. Career Pathways may incorporate Career Technical Education (CTE) but also enable graduates to continue in some form of postsecondary education, including four-year and two-year colleges and technical training. Any student can follow a Career Pathway; it is not reserved, as shop classes once were, for those deemed not to be college material. Nor is a Career Pathway a track leading only to one destination; it opens options and provides a sense of direction. One goal of Career Pathways is to answer the student's perennial question, "Why do we have to learn this?"

Career Pathways and PBL need not be combined, but PBL is well suited to the purpose. Students in CTE classes make things. PBL integrates the doing with academic as well as technical learning, having students document and reflect on their work. It also gives students more control over their learning and more responsibility for it. PBL activities impart many of the competencies valued by employers, thereby meeting students' needs to prepare for both further education and employment. PBL also connects schools with their communities. Students learn outside class. People from the community come into school as expert advisors and exhibition participants. Teachers make field trips and have externships with community organizations, notably workplaces. Both teachers and students benefit from interaction with adults from beyond the school world.

Educators who hope to answer Elmore's question, to seek real change at a scale that matters, need to answer (at least) two questions: What does good look like? and How do we make good big? Answering the first question entails access to examples of good practice. For PBL, HTH is one such: "not a model but an example," as people there like to say. As the stories below illustrate, examples are needed within a school too; teachers are motivated and guided by their peers' innovations. While we have not yet answered the second question satisfactorily, these stories shed some light on one way good ideas and practices spread: teachers and others in schools directly observe other teachers who are more experienced with PBL than they are. They participate in professional development (PD) that is well designed to inform and encourage them. With support from expert peers, from administrators, and from each other, they then try out PBL with their own students and invite others in their school to join them.

This approach to changing schools contrasts with more conventional top-down approaches. Teachers are accustomed to being told about change by administrators and instructed in how to make it by experts who have either never taught or are long out of the classroom. Because the average duration of a principal or a superintendent is three to four years, long-term teachers are often inured to their coming and going, knowing that they can patiently wait for the latest new initiative to blow over. Making it possible for teachers to learn from one another and to turn to their colleagues for advice and encouragement may look slower than issuing an edict but it is more likely to result in real and lasting change.

To illustrate some of the challenges of introducing PBL with a Career Pathways orientation into conventional schools, the author of each of the following chapters describes what has happened during the year or two preceding June 2017. The settings are California schools or school systems in two large metropolitan regions (Sacramento and San Diego), a small city (Downey), and two agricultural regions (Sonoma County and Boonville). One school enrolls mostly caucasian and middle class students; most have a majority of students of color who qualify for free and reduced-price lunches. One school system is for youth in the juvenile justice system. Each chapter was written by a teacher or former teacher at HTH, bringing their firsthand knowledge of PBL to their role as chroniclers of change in other schools.

How does change happen?

These stories respond to yet another question, containing parts of the previous questions: How do educators and schools make the change from traditional pedagogy to PBL? Two of the chapters are about the beginning phases of that change. Kali Frederick's account of Anderson Valley High School in Boonville, an agricultural community in Northern California, recounts the first steps taken by a team of teachers and one administrator who work together thoughtfully to build on prior instances of PBL in their school and respectfully to bring others along with them. Describing Warren High School in Downey, near Los Angeles, where teachers also worked hard to overcome the barriers to starting up, Stephanie Lytle notes the teachers' strategy of starting small and their capacity to learn from initial mistakes. "Momentum" is the name of the system of small schools that enroll youth in San Diego County's juvenile justice system. Lillian Hsu explains how field trips to a comparable school in Los Angeles and to a variety of schools in Boston inspired teachers to adopt PBL, agreeing to jump in and try it rather than to spend a long time planning.

PBL culminates in exhibition where students formally present what they have done and what they have learned to parents, other teachers, other students, and members of the broader community. Planning for an exhibition helps shape project design and anticipation of exhibition motivates students to do their best work. It also proves to be an effective device for attracting other teachers to adopt PBL. The team in Anderson Valley used exhibitions strategically in their plan to recruit their colleagues to use PBL. At Momentum, the first exhibitions of student learning energized teachers throughout the system and awed administrators and court officials, who had no idea the youth they worked with were capable of what they demonstrated. Even the exhibitions at Warren High School that were planned as small steps inspired other teachers to try PBL themselves.

Perhaps the strongest message of this book is that people don't make change on their own. The forms of support most prominently featured in the stories are teamwork, professional development, consultation, and encouragement from administrators. The purpose of the

Career Pathways PBL Leadership Academy was to inform and motivate educators to bring PBL to their schools. The Academy comprised two sessions of a rich PD experience, in the fall and spring of each year. The timing enabled teams from each school to return after their initial efforts to share, garner advice, and recharge. Each team was also assigned a mentor, an experienced HTH teacher who made site visits and was available by phone or video conference to respond to questions and share resources.

But support also came from other sources. Two specialists from the Sonoma County Office of Education were key supporters for the teachers Daisy Sharrock observed and interviewed. Those teachers also expressed their appreciation for the County Office's integrated pathway coaches who assisted them. In the CRANE Consortium of school districts in the Capital Region (Sacramento), Mike Amarillas found the Agriculture, Natural Resources & Food Production Coordinator had become "the PBL lady," who supports innovative educators in many schools with wisdom and energy. Teachers in Warren High School relied on the permission of administrators to deviate from the "pacing guides" adopted by their school, which their colleagues followed and thought they should follow too. The same administrators assured the pioneering teachers that mistakes are learning opportunities, not failures signaling that they should give up. By treating participating educators as a team representing their school or district, Academy organizers fostered continuing collaboration. As an example, the Anderson Valley team organized a PD event for their colleagues as an introduction to PBL.

This PD also illustrates another theme to the stories: teacher leadership. Teachers generally lack the kind of career ladder that other professions afford. Even a teacher who is recognized as outstanding can carry the same responsibilities and perform the same actions on the day before retirement as on her first day on the job. The only route to greater responsibility, higher status, and higher pay—beyond that for seniority—leads out of the classroom. The perverse results are that excellent teachers have an incentive to leave the classroom and if they choose to remain there then less-than-excellent teachers become administrators. These accounts demonstrate that if they have the time, financial resources, and authorization, teachers can band together to lead change in their school.[4]

The Career Pathways movement is a reconceptualization of CTE that incorporates postsecondary education as a step toward a career, what should be an obvious connection that is ignored by the separation of students into the college-bound and those predicted to go to work after high school graduation. As such it appropriately includes among its leaders veteran CTE teachers and specialists who know something about helping students prepare for their occupational futures and about teaching by engaging students in making things. The low status of CTE among the general public and in schools means that CTE educators are seldom in leadership positions. That bias tends to make CTE educators defensive. As a result, they have a habit of traveling with their wagons circled. It is refreshing to see CTE educators as change leaders, as in Anderson Valley where CTE teachers worked from the fringes to the core. CTE teachers and administrators also took leadership in Sonoma County, Warren High School, and the CRANE Consortium.

The concluding chapter on Momentum carries a compelling message: If PBL can flourish in schools for youth who are incarcerated or on parole, where student turnover is constant, then it can surely flourish in schools considered "regular." Some visitors to HTH hold that PBL may work for these students but would not for theirs. The more perceptive see that PBL does not depend upon students arriving with exceptional capabilities but on teachers who expect great things of their students and create the conditions in which they can meet those expectations. That is definitely the case in Momentum schools, where both teachers and students face extraordinarily trying circumstances. To paraphrase Frank Sinatra, if they can do PBL there, you can do it anywhere.

The following profiles of how schools shift toward PBL convey practical insights into how others can make this transition. They are honest and detailed enough to convey the gritty realities and uncertain progress that step-by-step manuals and idealized case studies leave out. The change efforts are successful enough to convince most readers that the effort is worthwhile. They are realistic enough to demonstrate that success is neither uniform nor guaranteed. Heroes inspire us but their deeds often seem unattainable. Courageous teachers in whom we can see some of ourselves are likely to be more helpful guides to changing our practices. Real teachers in real schools can do something like these teachers have done. If the stories in this book encourage and assist educators in making their schools and classrooms more equitable, more powerful and more engaging learning environments, then it will have achieved its authors' aims.

References and Resources

1   R. F. Elmore, "Getting to Scale with Good Education Practices," *Harvard Educational Review* 66 no. 1 (1996): 1–26.

2   S. B. Sarason, *The Culture of the School and the Problem of Change.* 2nd ed. (Boston: Allyn and Bacon, 1982).

3   National Research Council, *Education for Life and Work: Developing Transferable Knowledge and Skills in the 21st Century* (Washington, DC: National Academies Press, 2012); K. L. Zeiser, J. Taylor, J. Rickles, M. S. Garet, and M. Segeritz. "Evidence of Deeper Learning Outcomes: Findings from the Study of Deeper Learning, Opportunities and Outcomes," Report 3. Washington, DC: American Institutes for Research, 2014.

4   One of the distinctive features of HTH is the extent to which it gives teachers leadership opportunities, including as mentors and as designer and director of PD for teachers in other schools.

Lorilee Neisen, CRANE coordinator

Inspiration, Not Replication

The Work at Hand

Career and Technical Educators
at the Forefront of Deeper Learning

Mike Amarillas
High Tech High North County

In 2002, the Civil Rights Project of Harvard University identified Sacramento, California, as the most racially diverse city in the United States. That year in *TIME* magazine, Ron Stodghill and Amanda Bower wrote that "by 2059 at the latest, according to U.S. Census figures, there will no longer be a white majority in America. Sacramento, then, provides perhaps the clearest view into the nation's future—a glimpse into what our neighborhoods, schools, churches and police forces may look like just a few decades from now."[1] Stodghill and Bower's prediction holds up fifteen years later, as the diversity of both Sacramento and the nation continue to increase.[2]

The extreme heterogeneity of Sacramento extends beyond racial statistics and beyond the city limits. The greater Sacramento metropolitan area, or Capital Region, encompasses a sprawling landscape of rural communities and suburbs dotted with smaller urban centers like Davis and Yuba City. Dentists and physicians are on average the highest paid workers in the area's seven counties, but agriculture and construction loom large in the economy. The farming sector employs tens of thousands of people in the area and the fastest growing jobs through 2024 are predicted to be in ironwork, brickwork, flooring, and roofing.[3,4] Technology firms such as Intel, Apple, and Hewlett-Packard maintain a presence here, but there have been high-profile layoffs in recent years.[5,6] The Capital Region's economic landscape is varied and changing.

A cohort of career and technical educators is striving to better prepare their students to work in such a dynamic and diverse economy. With support from the state-funded consortium "Capital Region Academies for the Next Economy" (CRANE), these new and veteran teachers are seeking new professional development opportunities and implementing new project-based learning programs at their schools. They are pushing the envelope of career and technical education (CTE) beyond the rote and into the realm of contemporary "deeper learning."[7] As part-and-parcel of CTE, they demand real-life relevance for their curriculum and seek to give students career skills. CTE teachers already orient their practice towards authentic work and industry rather than academics, and they are beholden to relatively fewer content standards. Beginning in the framework of the classic CTE model (rather than a traditional academic one) has advantageously positioned these teachers to push their instruction towards the deeper learning outcomes. Regardless of their school's specific demographics or their program's infrastructure, the three teachers most closely examined in this piece find ways to give their students valuable deeper learning experiences and increase their students' chances at success in the 21st century economy.

Career Pathways

The CRANE consortium began in 2014 with the stated goal to "provide students in the Capital Region with rigorous academic and career pathways, which are linked to economic and labor market needs and trends, thus helping students to become the leading entrepreneurial workforce for the next economy."[8] At the most basic level, CRANE uses its California state funding to provide grants and teacher training for high school CTE programs. CRANE has six broad industry sectors of focus: Agriculture, Natural Resources and Food Production; Advanced Manufacturing, Engineering and Construction; Health and Biological; Information and Communication Technologies; Entrepreneurship and Finance; and Training and Transition. At a deeper level, CRANE functions primarily through the individual sector coordinators who tend community relationships to benefit CTE programs. These coordinators work to connect teachers with resources, create new professional development events, and provide personal on-site mentorship. CRANE and its coordinators serve dozens of schools, districts, and organizations in the Capital Region, from Yuba City in the north to Liberty Ranch in the south, and from Grass Valley in the east to Winters in the west.

Agriculture coordinator and self-described "PBL Lady" Lorilee Niesen traverses these nearly two thousand square miles of cities, suburbs, and farmland in a muddy Ford Super Duty, often with her five pound Yorkshire terrier, Hattie, as co-pilot. Lorilee wears her light brown hair to her shoulders and sweeps it from in front of her gray blue eyes often while in conversation. Her style—jeans, boots, close-cropped jacket, rustic necklace—alludes to her lifetime experience with agriculture (known simply as "ag" by many around here) and her home life on ranch land north of Sacramento. Nearly twenty-five years as a

CTE teacher and 4H advisor have made Lorilee an integral and respected member of the agricultural community in the Capital Region. As a CRANE coordinator, she works to support teachers implementing new programs and projects within the CRANE consortium. Thanks to CRANE's position outside of typical school or district structures, Lorilee operates as a neutral third party trusted and appreciated by teachers and administrators alike. Educators respond enthusiastically to her professional development offerings and reach out to her when they encounter difficulties with project-based learning (PBL). She prefers to work face-to-face and drives great distances daily to do so—she calls it simply "customer service":

> My very first part of the work was getting out and establishing those relationships with my teachers. Developing that trust, asking right off the bat, "What do you need? How can I make your job easier?" Because after 24 years in the classroom, I would have loved for someone to walk in and say, "What can I do for you?" Our model is customer service. We are here to serve our teachers.

Sometimes the service she offers is emotional rather than material. In the Super Duty one brisk February morning, Lorilee takes a speakerphone call from a local social science teacher who had hoped to host some visitors from San Diego's High Tech High. Audibly strained, the teacher says his team had not progressed enough with PBL and has nothing grand to show off. Lorilee is upbeat and encouraging. "Don't be embarrassed," she says, "Baby steps. Small projects and it will build on itself."

While her lengthy official title (Agriculture, Natural Resources & Food Production Coordinator) accurately conveys her background and initial focus, Lorilee's personal priority for CTE in the 21st century is interdisciplinary work. She describes framing a PBL workshop she organized.

> When we did the summer workshops we really encouraged schools to bring a team. And encouraged them not to just bring a team of CTE teachers, not to just bring a CTE teacher and an admin, but to bring a CTE teacher with academic teachers and really encourage that across disciplines. In education we have those silos... "Pillars of education" is what they call them. It's about breaking down those silos and having people work together... A lot of times in CTE students are labeled: "Those are your kids." They're not our kids, they're everyone's kids.

She gestures emphatically with pointed fingers, eyes wide, as she makes the point. In Lorilee's long history as an agriculture teacher she made deep personal connections and developed strong relationships with students; she was taken aback those times when other teachers would label them "agriculture students" and expect Lorilee to account for these students underperforming in their classrooms.

Lorilee rails against this notion that certain students belong best in certain classes, the notion that particular students belong under the purview of particular staff members, the notion of "your kids". The idea cuts two ways. Boxing in students as a particular type allows teachers to avoid the work of maintaining relationships with students ("Can you deal with Johnny? He's one of your kids") and allows teachers to act possessively with regards to students ("Why did you ask Claire to help with that? She's not one of your kids"). Putting up walls between disciplines encourages the building of walls between people. Lorilee gets the most satisfaction when

CRANE helps teachers bridge subject areas and connect their communities in constructive ways.

Deeper Learning

In the spirit of breaking down disciplinary walls, Lorilee has collaborated extensively with the other CRANE sector coordinators and with outside organizations. In 2016, Lorilee arranged for herself and a group of teachers to attend a professional development workshop at High Tech High, a network of public charter schools and home to the nation's first graduate school of education embedded inside of a K–12 school community. High Tech High's origins lie in Larry Rosenstock's work teaching carpentry and Rob Riordan's work on authentic internships, so the connection between PBL and career preparation is woven into the fabric of the organization. The multi-day institute in the spring of 2016 took place as part of High Tech High's Career Pathways PBL Leadership Academy.

High Tech High champions a vision for PBL connected to "deeper learning," a set of learning outcomes that research shows are highly relevant to 21st century economic success. Recent literature from the Hewlett Foundation and American Institute for Research have refined and structured the concept of deeper learning around these six core competencies:[9]

1. Master core academic content
2. Think critically and solve complex problems
3. Work collaboratively
4. Communicate effectively
5. Learn how to learn
6. Develop academic mindsets

The first of the competencies is traditionally academic—students must know the fundamental disciplinary content needed to access their chosen career. Beyond that first item, however, the deeper learning competencies encompass mostly interpersonal and intrapersonal skills that reside outside the usual disciplinary continuum. The High Tech High model devotes significant time and energy to developing these skills in addition to core content knowledge. The concept of deeper learning is fundamental and not some facet of PBL instruction. Rather, the advantage and relevance of PBL for 21st century students comes from how well PBL teaches deeper learning.

Unsurprisingly, High Tech High's interdisciplinary (Rob Riordan might say "anti-disciplinary") outlook resonated with Lorilee. Deeper learning connotes the sort of transferable skills that will serve students in the modern economy, dovetailing perfectly with CTE and the goals of CRANE. Lorilee set up a viewing of the documentary film, *Most Likely to Succeed*, which follows a High Tech High team through exhibition while contrasting the school's PBL model with traditional public education. More than 120 educators from throughout the Capital Region attended the screening.

Based on positive response and interest from teachers, Lorilee collaborated with High Tech High staff on a summer professional development workshop for educators who would be unable to attend a workshop in San Diego. Lorilee's two-day event, called "PBL: Making It Happen," was borrowed from High Tech High programming while also catering to the needs of Capital Region CTE teachers. Lorilee and her support team elected to begin professional development with a "project slice" or authentic hands-on experience, in this case a visit to local businesses to do some community research. Later Lorilee recalls:

> That was a blast! I had teachers literally say
> I've never gone to professional development

and gone on a field trip right off the bat. It was like, "Come in, get on the bus." Their only instruction was to wear comfortable shoes and bring a camera. Instead of walking in, sitting down, and then, "I'm going to deliver information and you're going to take it." We know what that traditional PD looks like.

Lorilee used the outside excursion as a jumping off point to have teachers discuss project structures, planning, and more.

That sort of unexpected shift in professional development, the opportunity to engage with work outside the classroom, sparked the interest of many teachers. Lorilee's workshop acted as a catalyst, prompting several teachers to begin deeper project work at the very next opportunity, in the fall of 2016. Melissa May of Inderkum High School began a broadcast media program by producing interdisciplinary videos. Marc Imrie of Granite Bay High School instituted new project structures in his student tech support program. Kevin Clancy of Foothill High School reoriented his school's sports medicine curriculum around project work. With financial support from CRANE and direct personal help from Lorilee and other coordinators, these CTE teachers have been empowered to innovate. An examination of their practice yields insights for educators of every stripe.

For two days in February 2017, Lorilee is taking a contingent of High Tech High visitors, including this author, on a whirlwind tour of multiple CRANE member schools. What follows is an attempt to capture in a glance the deeper learning blossoming at Inderkum, Granite Bay, and Foothill thanks to the passionate CTE teachers there.

Melissa May—Broadcasting at Inderkum High School

Students traverse a series of dim, low hallways to reach Melissa May's classroom. They pass by gray walls and underneath white ceiling panels until opening her door and revealing a burst of vibrant color. Half the room is painted aggressively green and lit up with a rig of stage lights. Three cameras, each looming on a tripod the size of a person, occupy central positions. One area has been set up like a news desk. Against this backdrop, Melissa May moves quickly, flitting from person to person and from conversation to conversation as she prepares her thirty-two students for a video shoot. Her indigo blue sweater and blonde pixie hairdo complement the bright surroundings. The fact that Melissa spent fourteen years hosting television at ABC10 Sacramento gives some indication of her age, but the exuberant woman dashing around the green screen classroom seems younger.

Melissa May brings both tremendous enthusiasm and vast broadcasting experience to Inderkum, her first teaching position. "In my high school they had a TV program and that really sparked my interest... I've been thinking about it for a while. I love doing career days, talking to students," she told colleagues during her farewell-from-broadcasting interview televised in March 2016. At that time, she had aspirations to give students useful skills and to ignite a spark for the work of broadcasting. Now, about one year since Melissa expressed those intentions on the air, a brief observation of her classroom reveals her vision made concrete. As the class period gets into full swing some students take their positions at the news desk, others conduct research or type scripts on computers, and one group goes to the adjacent "control room" to direct and monitor the imminent video shoot.

Inderkum High School is a comprehensive high school serving around 1900 students. Inderkum is located to

Melissa May, Inderkum High School

the northwest of Sacramento, within the city limits but in an area where suburban neighborhoods transition to farmland. The school is diverse along two axes. Half the student body is socioeconomically disadvantaged, as indicated by qualifying for the free or reduced-price lunch program. And the racial/ethnic makeup of the school has no majority—24% Black or African American, 24% Hispanic or Latino, 16% Asian, 14% White, 8% Filipino, 6% multiracial, and 3% Native Hawaiian or Pacific Islander. The school outperforms its district and the state on standardized tests of English Language Arts, but underperforms on math.

In the control room, a senior named Serina prepares the video chroma-key effect that transforms the background into any location imaginable. Looking through the window into the main classroom, she sees students at a table with a bright green wall behind them. Watching on the monitors instead, she sees those same students at the same table but with the school atrium behind them. With a mouse click, she swaps the background a few times to show the different options. Several other students observe her movements to learn the process for themselves. Thanks in part to her experience editing video footage for her personal basketball highlight reel, Serina is confident at the console and enjoys her role.

Outside in the classroom, Melissa continues coaching students as they prepare for today's video shoot—a "hot wings challenge" with students racing to see who can eat the most spicy chicken wings. She sends students to get hot sauce from the culinary class, prompts some students to set up cameras, and checks in with students about their scripts. An unexpected challenge pops up—the teleprompters are down so the news anchors will need to read from sheets of paper. Soon, an entire additional class of more than thirty students enters. These are Achim Dangerfield's chemistry students, who will collaborate with Melissa's broadcasting class to produce science videos; the "hot wings challenge" is to be the first. The broadcasting students have left gaps in the script for Achim's students to fill with research about the chemistry of spice and relevant measurements. Once the chemistry students have settled in, Melissa provides them with slips of paper to offer feedback about the video shoot. Soon, Serina announces on a loudspeaker, "Quiet on the set!" The crowded room falls silent and the news anchors begin to speak. The race to eat hot wings goes off without a hitch, though Melissa jokingly assures students that in the final version the spice level will be even higher.

Melissa and Achim hope to leverage the momentum of her broadcasting program to enhance student work in multiple content areas at Inderkum High School. Using Google classroom to manage logistics, Melissa and Achim collaborate across their school's departmental boundaries. At a large comprehensive school like this, with around two thousand students, they value any opportunity to connect staff or students. Eventually, they hope to implement videographic performance-based assessment in classes around the school. Melissa and Achim plan to build on the interest of many students who are already shooting, starring in, and editing their own social media video posts. With additional support from administrators and entities like CRANE, they see great potential in allowing students to express their mastery of content in a format they are already engaged in. Melissa believes educators can "meet students where they are" and give them avenues for learning that build on skills relevant to teenagers today.

As the CTE teacher of the duo, Melissa sees her role as providing concrete skills and a framework for creating quality products. She has worked with CRANE funds to renovate the broadcast room itself and build the capability for Inderkum students to make videos worth watching. The last year has required a huge investment of time, energy, and capital, but Melissa remains committed to the endeavor. She describes the value she sees in the hands-on project-based learning.

> I think that one of the big payoffs is the enthusiasm with the kids. It gets them out of their routine... For instance, [teaching] how to use a video camera—is it effective if I stand up there, even if I model how to do it? Or is it effective if we spend a little bit of time and then we actually get into small groups and we actually do it? I think it sticks and I think, especially in a big school, it plays to people's strengths that they can demo and show creatively how to make it work. Not just a standardized test, not just depending on language skill. I think it's accessible to all the students and I actually think it's more fun... You get a lot of buy-in from students.

As she speaks these words, multiple students mill about the room. They are spending their lunch time to create videos for Black History Month. Two students, Laura and Cynthia, arrived at school an hour early that morning to work on the project. This level of engagement, with voluntary participation beyond class time, occurs only when students have truly "bought in" and see value in the work they are doing. While Melissa May's current interdisciplinary project with chemistry is an achievement unto itself, the greater achievement is the concrete realization of her vision for student broadcasting. She created the Inderkum broadcasting studio and now it can serve as a vehicle for students' creativity.

Melissa has created an ecosystem bigger than a single project or class. Students will utilize the broadcasting resources available to them to create products she had not imagined. Already, she has compiled a YouTube channel, "Tiger Talk" (named for the Inderkum High mascot), containing dozens of videos conceptualized and executed entirely by students. The final form and scope of what students will produce is up to them. The broadcasting program serves as a conduit through which students can communicate in their own voice.

Participation in Melissa's CTE broadcasting program will build students' deeper learning competencies, communication first and foremost. The students do the broadcasting, not the teacher. The students must convey their message. Whether that message is about the chemical composition of spicy hot wings, Black History Month, or simply new school policies, the student broadcasters must make thoughtful decisions about how to communicate information. Students in broadcasting will grapple with questions of craft in the pursuit of clearer communication.

The other deeper learning competencies are embedded in the program as well. Depending on the video being produced, students must master certain content knowledge and incorporate it in their product. Students must incrementally solve the complex problem of turning their ideas into scripts or storyboards and eventually into proper footage. When disagreements and difficulties in their workflow pop up, which invariably happens, students must think critically about how to overcome the issue and move ahead. The projects students pursue are complicated enough that they are only feasible through collaboration, with a variety of different skill sets represented in the process. Students must communicate with each other and with Melissa about their needs, and, of course, the final product, the video itself, is a form of communication.

When creating videos about topics of their choosing, students must carry out the necessary research and seek

Critique

Giving and receiving feedback is an integral part of effective PBL. Students develop the deeper learning competencies of collaboration and communication by presenting their work and considering the work of others. Executing an effective project often necessitates continuing iteration, whether that means drafts of a written piece or prototype versions of a mechanical apparatus. Revision plays a role in Melissa May's CTE broadcasting program through multiple takes and editing. After students complete a run-through take of a video, Melissa solicits audience feedback about the actors' performances, staging choices, and video editing possibilities. Students from the audience share their thoughts with the whole class so that members of the relevant teams can take note and act on the feedback.

A secondary level of critique is also possible when students consider what constitutes good feedback. Blanket assessments of quality ("I like it") don't offer insights to the creator about how to improve. Too much negativity or personal attacks ("You did a bad job on his part") put the creator on the defensive and distract from meaningful conversation. High Tech High encourages critique to focus on the content rather than the creator and for the feedback to be kind, specific, and helpful in its phrasing ("I think that part of the broadcast would be more effective if we used B-roll but we keep the speaker's audio."). This leads to constructive feedback that all students can use to improve their work, focuses on important learning targets, and maintains a constructive classroom culture.

out new resources. They receive some basic training, but they are expected to read online and learn from one another about using the wide variety of video production tools at their disposal. Students see tangible results to their efforts as the Tiger Talk videos improve in quality, and they start to develop confidence in both their new-found abilities and their capacity for self-improvement. Every time broadcast students create a video that other students watch, they collectively build the school culture and community connections. When student videos are utilized by other classes for instructional purposes, it emphasizes how various modes of work can serve academic ends. The product through which a student demonstrates mastery of academic content does not itself have to be academic, so that the skills of something like videography can be used to showcase expertise in a particular content area like chemistry. As students work to craft their final product, they simultaneously grapple with the disciplinary content.

Students who achieve success in Melissa May's class will undoubtedly acquire a set of technical broadcasting competencies. Students might even develop an interest in the field as an option for their future, just as Melissa did when her high school TV class ignited her own passion. More important, however, students who succeed in broadcasting at Inderkum High School will have built the deeper learning competencies of critical thinking, collaboration, and communication. They will be better prepared to tackle complex problems that require self-directed learning. Melissa May helps students become more marketable, more confident, and more entertaining.

Marc Imrie—Information Technology at Granite Bay High School

Students and teachers are familiar with Marc Imrie's CTE class even if they don't know the name Marc

Imrie. Granite Bay's information technology class, GBiT (pronounced "gee bit"), serves as the high school's tech support. Students run every aspect of the system, from the digital management of support request tickets to visiting teachers and staff in person throughout the school. The enterprise operates out of a cavernous classroom near a back corner of campus, where ductwork and vents painted in the school colors descend from above like stalactites. The bulk of the room contains a half dozen rows of computers, enough for all the thirty-something students even though less than half are seated there. Some do move from workstation to workstation, looking over one another's shoulders and pointing at screens. Others work along the perimeter of the room refurbishing equipment and retrieving supplies, while still others come and go on tech support visits. Marc Imrie has a standing-height desk near the center of the room, the calm at the eye of the storm. He looks trim in a short-sleeved button-down shirt and gestures emphatically as he speaks. He never set out to be a tech support guru. "I got this position because I was the problem solver. I was a history teacher before, and for ten years at my last site we didn't have a tech person on campus and I became that go-to tech guy."

During the class period, Marc meets with familiar guests from High Tech High and CRANE, as well as a few school and district staff. All the students engage with the work of tech support in its various forms, with necessary management decisions dispensed by the "student director," Brian. A senior currently in limbo awaiting college admissions decisions, he has risen through the ranks of GBiT since taking Introduction to Computer Science as a freshman. That course is the only strict prerequisite for the tech support program, but prospective students must also show initiative and skill. Last year, more fifty students applied for approximately thirty spots. Brian and the "student managers" communicate with Marc about the number of tech support openings to be filled and identify

Marc Imrie, Granite Bay High School

Inspiration, Not Replication

students who show both promising technical proficiencies and an enthusiastic attitude toward the work. Marc and the student leaders hold interviews before making a final decision. The hierarchy and enrollment process are intentionally business-like.

Says Marc,

> This class really demonstrates what [CTE] should look like. We have curriculum but it's not as structured as you would see in maybe a traditional course or even some other CTE courses. We've got teams of students who work from tech support, tech training, tech innovation, web development, marketing development. Each of those teams has a manager that manages that group and they all serve a different purpose, a role in serving the campus. We have a mission statement that talks about [how] the purpose of our class is to serve the community. It's real world in that they set their own goals and objectives, and they work with their own manager and team to set those goals. They work in a three-week cycle, called the "sprint cycle," towards those goals and objectives, and they're evaluated at the end by their manager and themselves as to whether they accomplished those training, service, and task goals. Similar to a workplace, where you're working on a team, you have a supervisor or manager, a task you're trying to complete. You work with your team and yourself to accomplish that goal. So [GBiT] is very real world."

Perhaps in a mirroring of the real world, GBiT struggles to attract female students. There are two female students in the room at the moment, versus dozens of males. Brian and the other student managers are sensitive to the issue but perplexed about what to do. More female students take the prerequisite introduction to computer science class, but enroll in Advanced Placement computer science rather than the tech support CTE class. Says one student manager, "AP Computer Science pulls from a larger audience just because of the AP element to it. A lot of people are going for the max GPA thing." Brian says, "That's the thing about this campus, if you put two letters in front of a course name, 'AP' or 'IB', then people want to take that class. They want a 4.9 GPA. That's just the culture of our campus."

Granite Bay exhibits an achievement-focused culture commonly associated with privileged high school programs. Nestled among gated communities twenty miles northeast of downtown Sacramento, just 11% of the school's student body is socioeconomically disadvantaged. The racial demographics are slightly more varied—68.4% White, 11% Hispanic or Latino, 9% Asian, 7% multiracial, 2% Filipino, and less than 2% Black or African American. Granite Bay outperforms its district and the state on every standardized test listed on their school accountability report card. Tensions at the school arise not from strife between constituent groups, but from the mercilessly competitive traditional track to college. The 2016 valedictorian used his graduation speech as a platform to criticize the school's focus on GPA and decry the school culture that allowed him to achieve the highest honors while never deeply connecting with his classmates or school community.[10]

In many ways, Marc Imrie's CTE program is the authentic counterpoint to the GPA-chasing academic culture. Rather than quantitative success, Marc encourages qualitative personal improvement such as clearer communication and confident interactions with the adult world. Instead of building traditional content expertise, he hopes to foster students' deeper learning competencies. He says:

I hope they're developing what are referred to as soft skills: the ability to self-manage, to set truly challenging goals for themselves, to work towards those goals, to time-manage, to problem solve, to follow through, to evaluate their progress and successes and failures, to reflect on those.... Technical skill is one thing. They need certain tech skills and they need a foundation of knowledge. We try to support students in that foundation of technology. But more importantly, it's the soft skills. Do they know how to do troubleshooting, problem-solving? Are they setting goals for themselves to push themselves?"

Solving complex problems and addressing complex goals lie at the heart of GBiT, as modern tech support demands it. Staff requests for help span a variety of issues related to wifi connectivity, software installation, classroom audiovisual connections, and website maintenance. The small student teams respond to some particular domain of problems, with teams rotating continuously so that in one semester a student will field service requests in multiple domains. Once a small team has a request in their inbox, they gather the necessary resources and then send a delegate or two for the support visit proper. Depending on what the visit demands, students end up employing a variety of tools and techniques to solve the staff member's problem.

Student director Brian says that the biggest challenge facing GBiT students is the personal interaction with the teacher as a client. Marc agrees, and works tirelessly to develop students' collaborative and communicative skills for that purpose.

We start the semester talking about customer service. We talk about what a company even is: A company is something that offers a service or a product that people want. Somebody determines there is value in that product. Whether it's Apple or it's Pewdiepie (you know, he's gaming on YouTube, makes millions of dollars) there's value in a company and its perceived, perceived value, that's all it is. How do you, as a potential employee or business owner, develop a product or a skill that other people want or see value in? Part of that is the way you approach people, how you interact, how you talk to them, how you sell yourself. Can you present a product in a way that somebody else says, "Ah, I like that idea, I want that"? Or "I like your service, and the way you interact with me, and I would hire you to help solve my problems." So we talk customer service, we do some role play with customer service. Something as simple as how you enter a classroom, how you interact with the teacher, how you follow up, you offer additional services, all of those things are going to make you stand out above the majority of students who don't know how to interact.... Students getting the opportunity to serve customers is new for them. Sending them out to go help a teacher solve a problem, that's totally role reversal for most high school students. Most high school students it's [the] teacher telling them what to do and how to do it, and then [solving their] problem like "I don't understand this concept, tell me how to do it." In this class, the teacher needs the student to solve the problem.

The authentic demand from teachers and class structures built around professional practices have made student tech support a major success. Students are empowered

Interdisciplinary Work

When Lorilee Niesen speaks of breaking down the "silos of education," the University of California college acceptance requirements give some sense of what those specific silos are—math, English, history, science, and the arts. Universities and teacher credentialing programs tyically separate these domains—for their students and also in teacher training programs—and the subsequent experience of students is one that is fragmented among several disciplinary categories. CTE teachers tend to occupy a space outside this tradition, thanks to their grounding in career work rather than academic discipline. Many careers in the twenty-first century span different academic disciplines by nature, positioning CTE teachers to push student learning beyond disciplinary boundaries.

When students in Marc Imrie's GBiT program need to solve a problem with a classroom audio system, for instance, they must read the request and conduct their own investigation to interpret the nature of the problem, consult written information online or in printed manuals, make measurements, do the technical repair work, and listen to the audio signal to assess the sound quality. And, the entire experience takes place in a social context, as they report to classmates about their progress and work with adults in several places on campus. Such a complex task may involve mathematical, linguistic, scientific, technical, and artistic skills. Students participating in Melissa May's broadcasting program can turn their cameras on any subject matter, enabling interdisciplinary collaboration with students and teachers across the school. Rather than being contained in a silo, a high quality video production or GBiT collaboration transcends content area.

with huge responsibility in return for holding themselves to high standards of personal conduct and technical skills. Taking inspiration from Google's famous "20% time," when employees have their time officially allocated to pursue personal interest projects, Marc has broadened the scope of GBiT by having students spend one day a week pursuing something of their own choosing.

> They develop their product, they argue its value in their proposal, they write a deliverables timeline of how they're going to get from point A to point Z to the product or service, and then they work on it every Friday. At the end they do a presentation on their process. Not so much their product because many of them don't get to the outcome they had intended, which is fine, it's a short period of time, but they talk about the process. How did they decide what was valuable? What customers were they targeting in their project? Who would actually pay for their service or product or whatever? How did they learn what they needed to learn? I'm not standing up here teaching them how to program their LED lighted shoes, they're finding the resources and materials, the tutorials they need. And if they have a product, they'll present it.

One project from last semester, a cell phone repair service, went so well that the GBiT student founder has continued advertising and operating the venture as a small business. Marc recounts the story of another student whose project doing web development for a flight simulation software company went so well that the student graduated early to accept a full-time position. Marc hesitates a bit in telling this tale, as he would prefer that students get college degrees before entering the workforce, but he understands the draw of real meaningful work. He hopes that his CTE program will lead to proactive, empowered workers in the world.

> The hope is the pathway would lead towards employees who aren't just your status quo, show up to work and do their thing. It should lead to people who have greater aspirations and see something more than punching the timeclock or just participating in a company. I want students who see bigger than that. They can impact whatever they end up working for or building. If it's their own company, they can influence that company. They can do it for the benefit of their own family or for the benefit of society and moving us forward as civilization. These bigger things. It's not just about going to work. Yeah you can be a programmer that programs the next messaging app that's the latest and greatest messaging app. Or there's programmers out there doing what I consider valuable work—in the medical industry, curing diseases, advancing manufacturing and safety, security—things that are going to make our lives better. I would hope that [students] see that from my program, the ability to influence or impact things on a bigger level.

Kevin Clancy—Sports Medicine at Foothill High School

Thanks to recent rain, the athletic fields at Foothill High look lush and green, visible from the school's open-air pathways. The school opened in 1965 and some of the buildings show their age, both inside and out. Track coach and sports medicine teacher Kevin Clancy has propped open the door to his classroom to welcome students and visitors inside. With light blonde hair and sharp features accentuated by a chinstrap beard, he remains fit from his college career as a distance runner. This is just his second

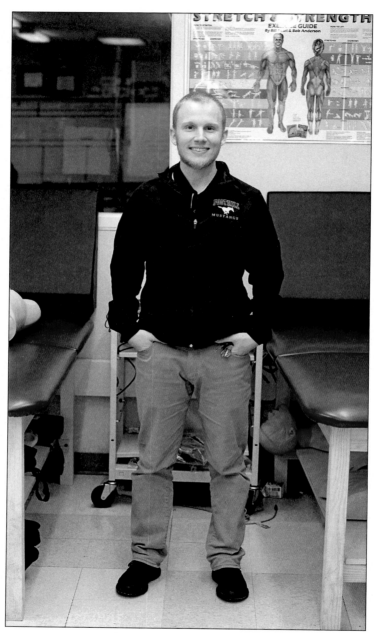

Kevin Clancy, Foothill High School

Inspiration, Not Replication

year of teaching and coaching at Foothill, and he has attacked his new roles with fervor. He answers questions about his program with a buzzing energy, nodding emphatically, excited to describe his strategies and show visitors resources around his classroom. The room is split into a distinct front and back end. The front end has a whiteboard and pull-down projector screen with tables and chairs arranged in two rough semi-circles facing the screen. The back end has two medical exam tables, a balance trainer, and a few other pieces of vintage medical and athletic equipment. Students file in and take their seats at the desks. In stark contrast to the aging facilities, the athletic students entering the room look at their peak. Several of them tower over the young "Coach Clancy," who greets the class warmly.

Foothill High School serves over one thousand students in a relatively densely populated neighborhood of Sacramento called Foothill Farms. Only eight miles distant from Granite Bay, the semi-rural area feels worlds away. The student body is 75% socioeconomically disadvantaged and the school is diverse—37% Hispanic or Latino, 31% White, 19% Black or African American, 4% Asian, 3% multiracial, and less than 2% Native Hawaiian or Pacific Islander. Standardized testing reveals varied results. Foothill performs comparably to its district at English language arts, but still below the state. Foothill underperforms the district and state dramatically at math and science. This is a challenging academic backdrop to the beginning of a career in education. Kevin was invigorated by his experiences with Lorilee of CRANE and the leadership academy at High Tech High. Upon returning to Foothill, he immediately began trying out new PBL strategies. He tells Lorilee and some other visitors, "The idea was that they would just begin working together. Even if it was informal, just working together."

The work happening today in Kevin's sports medicine class stays true to that collaborative drive. Where the existing curriculum calls for basic use of the textbook and some teacher-centered lectures, Kevin is breaking students into teams and assigning groups to different sections of the main text. In a jigsaw format, students will present on their groups' sections so that eventually students are exposed to the entirety of the relevant text. The simple twist on tradition excites Kevin and offers new chances for student personalization. His eyes get wide as he describes his rationale to the visitors:

> Let's take a chapter out of the book and let's start with that as our basis and let's grow from there. Let's create a presentation for the class that has [information from the text], but then you're going on researching outside sources. You know, they love using their phones so use your phone, research outside sources, use the laptops, go to the library! [The librarian] would love to have you down there and show her sports medicine collection. So basically, create presentations on what we're covering in class but integrate that [with] outside research. The idea of finding something new, bringing something new to the class that's not already there.

Kevin introduces the presentation prompts to the groups, cold-calling students by name to read instructions. Then, he spends the lion's share of class time floating from group to group and advising. Most have specific questions about things they encounter in the text. Others have questions about what constitutes outside research. The sports medicine program at Foothill has historically placed emphasis on the core academic content of the field, mostly kinesthesiology and biology. Through strategies like the jigsaw presentations, Kevin works to address that content in a way that also builds students' deeper learning competencies. At a few points he has flirted with even larger deviations from tradition.

> They got into personal training with some of the students on campus. The PE teacher sixth period gave us four students to go down to the weight room and work with. So they got to go through movement analysis, setting up baseline goals, baseline performance assessments—how many push-ups can you do? How many sit-ups can you do? Then they came back to the classroom and worked on a training program to get them better. So every time they had their program and they'd go down and work with them. You're literally seeing results, week to week you test them and you see that they've get better. There's a connection between the work you put in here and the work they've put in working out, and it's gotten them better.

For all his passion about folding PBL into his CTE program, Kevin remains somewhat hesitant about learning experiences that draw his students outside the classroom. He understands the possible value and enjoyed his own experience during Lorilee's professional development "field trip" last summer, but finds that students don't "quite know how to respond" when they're outside the classroom environment. He has succeeded at arranging meaningful project work and outlining clear objectives for these excursions, but finds his students behave somewhat unpredictably outside of his normal classroom routines. Even with an extensive preface, Kevin says, "they have trouble focusing the same way they would in class." This makes it hard for Kevin to feel as effective as a teacher.

> It was a little trouble for me to get out there and try to manage everything at the same time

and so I'm perfecting that. I'm not going to get away from that, I want to keep doing that because they're creating great products. But, you know, have it a little more focused. Just so that they're all on task…. That's something I'm working on, a better way to structure it.

On this day, CRANE Health and Biological Coordinator Darrell Parsons advises Kevin on techniques for working with students in these outside-the-classroom situations. Darrell reminds Kevin that he doesn't "have to figure out all the mysteries of the world" on his own and that Kevin can bring students' help into addressing the issue. Darrell encourages Kevin to have an honest conversation with students about the program's goals for them and the quality of their work outside the classroom. Devoting instructional time to talking about student behavior will push them to reflect about the purpose of the outside work and the impact of their own conduct.

Kevin's difficulties speak to the need for PBL teachers to manage students outside a conventional teaching setting. Kevin expertly manages his classroom via clearly stated objectives, smooth cold-calling, and physical presence among students. However, these techniques function less effectively when students are not seated close together in organized groups. Even CTE programs, which can look so different from academic core classes, tend to happen in purpose-built rooms. Putting students in the right frame of mind to do outside work takes time because it happens best when students have a shared understanding of why they're doing the work. They need to understand how they represent their fellow students and their teacher. Sending students into the wild, as in Marc Imrie's GBiT program, takes a huge leap of faith in student's willingness to conduct themselves appropriately and requires a culture where students take pride in their membership in the program. Running the sports medicine program at

Personalization

Students deeply engaged in PBL have must express their own voices and make choices about their learning. In the CTE programs supported by CRANE, student voice and choice appear in ways that reflect the particular technical domain at hand. In Melissa May's broadcasting program, students make creative and technical decisions at multiple stages in the process of producing a video. From the content to the script to the staging to the editing, every step is driven by students, including holding one another to high standards of quality. In Marc Imrie and Kevin Clancy's classes, there are fewer aesthetic choices to be made—fixing problems with Internet connectivity and human biology require students to behave in consistent, dependable ways and do not initially seem to afford as much space for creativity. Marc and Kevin incorporate student voice and choice in other ways. Marc has GBiT students create their own innovative products and launch on-campus businesses during 20% of their course time each week that is dedicated to their free choice. Kevin has his students partner with student-athletes at Foothill High School to learn about their needs to craft and continually improve customized workout plans to improve performance or ensure safe recovery from injuries.

Students become engaged in similar content and skills through different avenue; in PBL personalization is not self-paced learning, but rather achieving a personal relationship with the project. In the CTE programs described here, student engagement is directed toward pursuits with real-life relevance that can serve students long into their future careers.

Foothill, Kevin is at the early stages of making that leap and establishing that culture.

Eight to ten of Kevin's more advanced students serve as junior athletic trainers for Foothill's sports teams. They help athletes tape up, stretch, and more. Each one is certified in CPR and first aid in case of emergency. The teams come to rely on their help, and when one sports season ends another team is waiting to snatch up the newly available student trainer. These students have also visited local colleges to tour the schools and meet with professional sports medicine practitioners. After today's class, a few students stick around to spend their own lunchtime speaking with High Tech High and CRANE guests about life after high school.

Nolan, a broad-shouldered young man with a beaming smile, tells the visitors that he sees sports medicine as both a viable career option and an enjoyable high school course to simply explore. "I'm unsure of my major, so whatever I get in contact with, if I like it, maybe I'll move towards that. I don't have a set path...see what I like." He talks about how much values the chance to tour colleges through sports medicine and admits many of his peers haven't been able to do that through normal school classes.

Christina, a slight young lady with a crop of curly dark hair, has an important decision to make in the coming months. She wants to attend university to study either writing or athletic training. "I feel like anything I do it's going to be a straight path. If it's writing, go straight for it. Or if it's sports medicine, go straight for it." She agrees with one of the visitors from High Tech High that rich experiences in athletic training could make for quality writing material—either way she appreciates having these options.

Much like his students, Kevin still has decisions to make about where he wants to go. His grand vision for his program is still being drafted.

> The end goal? I'm still trying to figure out what that is. I'm kind of a planner, I always think about the end goal, but with sports medicine here there's a lot of uncontrollables so I'm trying to take it day-to-day. I'm trying to figure out where to go. I'm hoping that by the end my end goal will be clearer. You've got to work with where you are first. You can have an end goal but if your reality is somewhere over here your end goal might not be appropriate.

Kevin and his advanced students see promise in starting a competition for high school sports medicine students. There are college-level events involving wrapping ankles or other joints in the shortest time, then having the result inspected and scored. Nolan and Christina love the sound of this, and can't resist showing the day's visitors some wrapping techniques on the exam tables in the back of the room. With deft movements they immobilize the ankles of two classmate volunteers, one of whom doesn't pause her studying from a biology text. Nolan and Christina certainly look ready to compete.

Whatever next steps Kevin and his students take, Foothill's sports medicine program as it stands has given these students a chance to hone their deeper learning competencies, particularly collaboration. Kevin's students work on complex problems like the personal training plans, they communicate via presentations, they connect personally with the athletes under their care, they direct their own learning when doing research, and

Equity

CTE courses can ameliorate social issues of inequity in school by granting students of varying backgrounds the same access to success. CTE courses without prerequisites can admit students with all levels of prior academic achievement. When offered as elective courses, CTE classes are likely to have students from different grade levels working together. Often, CTE allows for extended hands-on project work that has multiple access points (i.e. ways for students to become excited about the course content). Kevin Clancy's sports medicine students, for instance, span three grade levels from sophomores to seniors. Some have high overall grade-point averages and others do not. In the coursework there are opportunities to weave in content related to athletics, biology, math, and physics, as well as communication skills and important lessons in teamwork and empathy.

These characteristics of CTE sync up with what High Tech High's Jeff Robin identifies as the equity-boosting traits of general PBL. Jeff states that "all students have a wide range of experiences and skill sets that can draw them into a project" and that teachers should set up their classrooms to honor this variety rather than expect all students to have identical competencies. Compared to traditional academic skills, he says, "making, doing, and collaborating are the skills that bring people together." The CTE programs supported by CRANE, and the shift toward PBL that they are facilitating, offer students many chances to make, do, and collaborate.

they experience how the academic work of understanding sports medicine concepts can better their real-life performance as student trainers.

Endless Opportunities

Lorilee Niesen, the CRANE coordinator who brought this author to visit Sacramento, feels tremendous pride in what teachers like Melissa May, Marc Imrie, and Kevin Clancy are accomplishing. An intimate sense of community permeates the CRANE schools, cultivated by the teachers and coordinators who work tirelessly to help their students thrive in the future. These educators know one another personally and strive to support one another in the ongoing pursuit of deeper learning. Their connection is a requisite for their endeavor, as transforming CTE into vibrant 21st century PBL will take time, effort, collaboration, and iteration. Lorilee says one salient hurdle is a particular mindset among teachers, "the mentality of 'we're going to meet today, we're going to develop the project, we're going to get the lesson plans done' and they think they're going to be able to complete project-based learning in one day." Lorilee wants teachers to understand that quality education comes with missteps and that organizations like CRANE exist to support them through challenges. When educators work together, opportunities for deeper learning in the CTE context are endless.

Comprehensive high schools would do well to identify the successful project-based aspects of their current CTE programs and expand on them. Many CTE teachers already operate programs that are tailored to their local situation and their own personal strengths while simultaneously remaining firmly connected to students' real economic prospects. Such programs offer virtually ideal circumstances for developing deep and enriching PBL. Core content teachers are often encouraged to lay out daily academic and language objectives to track incremental progress, whereas CTE teachers may already have students engaged in long-term hands-on work with objectives that may shift as the project progresses. They are primed to reframe their work as a deeper learning enterprise. The schools visited for the writing of this piece all fit this template: CTE resources existed at the school, a passionate teacher became involved, and now a boost from CRANE is enhancing the potency of the program. Students in these programs will have continued access to open-ended, collaborative, and communicative experiences that will prepare them for the world beyond high school.

Given this strong connection between CTE and PBL, most CTE teachers' input on issues relevant to students' lifelong success may be severely underutilized. Most teachers in the US have a master's degree or higher,[11] suggesting a highly academic slant to the current national educational framework. The deeper learning competencies, being oriented towards transferrable skills that grant economic success, are strikingly different from core content standards. It is fitting that the combination of CTE with deeper learning has arisen as a cutting-edge antidote to contemporary educational problems when the reasoning behind them is so similar to arguments for CTE from decades past. In November 1961, President John F. Kennedy convened industry experts to analyze the state of vocational education. After one year of research, the Panel of Consultants on Vocational Education released their final report.

> The Panel's general recommendations are that, in a changing world of work, vocational education must:
> - Offer training opportunities to... graduates who will enter the labor market
> - Provide training or retraining for the

millions of workers whose skills and technical knowledge must be updated, as well as those whose jobs will disappear due to increasing efficiency, automation, or economic change.

- Meet the critical need for highly skilled craftsmen and technicians through education during and after the high school years.
- Expand vocational and technical training programs consistent with employment possibilities and national economic needs.
- Make educational opportunities equally available to all, regardless of race, sex, scholastic aptitude, or place of residence.
- The Panel believes that the federal government must continue to work with states and local communities to develop and improve the skills of its citizens.[12]

These findings from 1962 echo the rationale for starting CRANE in 2014. This nearly 60 year-old passage evokes a connection between classic CTE and contemporary deeper learning. While these findings do not enumerate the deeper learning competencies, they suggest that workers of the era needed a new skill set for the times. In the 21st century, workers also need a new skill set to succeed in higher education and beyond. Then as now, students need to be prepared for an economy that will change as they engage with it. In this shifting world, the most valuable skills can transfer from context-to-context as circumstances change; the deeper learning competencies are precisely those skills.

Back in her office just southeast of Sacramento, Lorilee sits down with visitors from High Tech High to discuss CRANE. She shares many of the insights included in this piece, speaking animatedly about deeper learning, the

Exhibition

Lorilee Niesen sees exhibition as a next step for the CRANE partners. The accomplishments of students and teachers can go unseen by the larger community if efforts are not made to showcase the work. There are certainly some "high-visibility" aspects of the CTE programs described in this piece. Melissa May's student videos are posted online and viewed schoolwide. Marc Imrie's GBiT students appear all over campus and interact with non-GBiT staff daily. Kevin Clancy's student athletic assistants become fixtures of their sports teams. In all these cases, students' achievements are seen by a larger part of the school community than just the teacher and that period's classmates. This is certainly an improvement over classes where student work is submitted to the instructor and never seen by the world at large.

However, these programs still need opportunities for parents and outside community members to witness what students do. This can be more than a chance for parents to admire their child's work. Adult professionals can attend and offer feedback from an expert perspective. Ultimately, student work is "exhibited" in a context of service in the community—students' projects are inherently useful in the world beyond school. An authentic exhibition raises the social stakes and increases the perceived legitimacy of the work. Melissa May is creating a video showcase event, Marc Imrie wants to grow a student internship component to GBiT, and Kevin Clancy is working to create a sports medicine skills and knowledge competition judged by athletic trainers from local colleges.

teachers she supports, their innovative programs, and the next steps for PBL practices. As her CTE teachers do an increasingly effective job addressing the deeper learning competencies, she hopes to see their students' work made more visible to a larger audience through exhibition. She wants to celebrate all the CRANE partners have achieved, knowing that the act of putting work on display feeds back positively into the quality of the programs. After the interview, a photographer asks Lorilee to pose for a picture "wherever you're normally working." Lorilee laughs. This office is not the environment where she accomplishes her greatest work. The community feels her impact out in the partner schools where she meets with teachers and observes students in action. She poses for the photo standing in front of a desk where she seldom sits. Lorilee and the CTE teachers of CRANE know the future of education is not sitting behind a desk. The future of education is real work in the field.

References and Resources

1   Stodghill, Ron, and Amanda Bower, "Welcome to America's Most Diverse City," *Time*, August 25, 2002, http://content.time.com/time/nation/article/0,8599,340694,00.html.

2   "The White Population: 2010," U.S. Census Bureau, September 2011, https://www.census.gov/prod/cen2010/briefs/c2010br-05.pdf.

3   "Sacramento County Profile," California Employment Development Department, http://www.labormarketinfo.edd.ca.gov/

4   "California Agricultural Employment 2015 Annual Average," California Employment Development Department, http://www.labormarketinfo.edd.ca.gov/file/agric/ca-ag-employ-map-2015.pdf.

5   "Tech Companies," Greater Sacramento Economic Council, https://www.selectsacramento.com/sectors-industries/tech-companies/.

6   Victor Patton, "Hewlett Packard Layoffs Underline Problems in Sacramento's Tech Sector," *Sacramento Business Journal*, November 22, 2016, http://www.bizjournals.com/sacramento/news/2016/11/22/hewlett-packard-layoffs-underline-problems-in.html.

7   "What About Deeper Learning," Alliance for Excellent Education, http://deeperlearning4all.org/about-deeper-learning.

8   Capital Region Academics for the Next Economy (CRANE), https://www.cranepathways.org/.

9   "Deeper Learning Competencies," William and

Flora Hewlett Foundation, April 2013, http://www.hewlett.org/wp-content/uploads/2016/08/Deeper_Learning_Defined__April_2013.pdf.

10   Josh Tolley, "Valedictorian Shocks World with Brutally Honest Graduation Speech," YouTube video, 5:42, posted May 31, 2016, https://www.youtube.com/watch?v=a5uqNhfNHL8.

11   "Fast Facts," National Center for Education Statistics, https://nces.ed.gov/fastfacts/display.asp?id=28.

12   "Education for a Changing World of Work: Report of the Panel of Consultants on Vocational Education," U.S. Department of Health, Education, and Welfare, 1963, http://files.eric.ed.gov/fulltext/ED019500.pdf.

Katie Chesbro, Elsie Allen High School

Inspiration, Not Replication

Forging Connections
Supporting Authentic Learning in Sonoma County

Daisy Sharrock
High Tech High Graduate School of Education
Center for Research on Equity & Innovation

"**B**efore I knew it, it was summertime and I was walking through a homeless encampment in Santa Rosa."

Katie Chesbro was in her first year teaching world history at Elsie Allen, a large comprehensive high school in south Santa Rosa, California, when Dan Bartholome, the public safety teacher, asked her to collaborate to plan a cross-disciplinary project. Katie had no idea how they could combine their respective curriculums in a meaningful way, but confessed that as a first year teacher, she didn't feel like she could say no. And despite the muddy, ambiguous beginnings to their teaching partnership, she's glad she didn't.

Katie and Dan participated in a summer externship program set up by the Sonoma County Office of Education (SCOE). The week long immersive experience was designed to help teachers connect their course content to the surrounding community, and in the process, help their students see a place for themselves beyond the school walls too. The externship experience is part of a bigger network of support structures designed by SCOE to overcome the barriers between students and the adult world they will soon help create.

The Barrier Between Youth and Their Community

In the United States a student drops out of high school every 26 seconds. That's more than 1.2 million students every year.[1] Even students who stay in high school and do well, report feeling disengaged. In fact, by junior year, only 32% of students report feeling engaged in school.[2] What accounts for the massive disconnect between young people and our educational institutions? And why are we failing to convince them that the schooling they're engaged in is critical for their future success? According to the students of Santa Rosa, California, the problem is simple: what they're learning doesn't connect them to the world they see around them. It doesn't feel relevant at all.

Unfortunately, the educational experiences in most schools are ill-matched to the future schools purport to train young people for. A focus almost exclusively on content acquisition has replaced the largely experiential process of social maturation that prevailed a century ago. As a result, young people have lost early opportunities to experience the world of adult work, or to see a place for themselves in it.

How can educators break down the barriers that separate young people from the world they will inherit? What experiences can we create to prevent the current state of widespread disengagement? How can we help students understand the vast opportunities now available to them for their futures? These are the questions that keep Chuck Wade and Jessica Progulske from SCOE up at night.

The Systemic Barrier of Prior Experience

The separation of young people from adult work experiences is exacerbated by the systemic formation of a teaching force that emerges mainly from a formal schooling environment. The current education system is perfectly designed to produce teachers who can reproduce the status quo. Most teachers have only ever experienced traditional education institutions. Moreover, many of them were successful in school environments. Teachers often become teachers because they liked how they learned in school and their school experience, all 16 years of it, has trained them beautifully to develop and deliver lectures on content they personally find interesting. Unfortunately, teaching is possibly the last profession on earth where this skill could still be considered useful. Listening to a lecture in order to memorize and regurgitate facts does not help young people gain a deep appreciation for the nuances of designing experiments as a scientist, and finding the answers to the questions at the end of the chapter doesn't prepare students to think critically about the world around them so that can actively engage in civil society. Teachers unintentionally perpetuate the continued separation of young people from the broader community by providing the same experiences they had in school – direct instruction of content in the quest for individual cognitive achievement.

Chuck & Jessica:
The Quest for Authentic Learning Experiences

The divide between students in Sonoma county schools and the surrounding community is not lost on Chuck Wade, SCOE's Program Coordinator for Career Technical Education. Former multimedia design teacher and long time Sonoma County resident, Chuck is passionate about bringing more authentic experiences into more classrooms more of the time.

Chuck Wade and Jessica Progulske,
Sonoma County Offfice of Education

Inspiration, Not Replication

He recalls a particularly memorable valedictorian speech from Casa Grande, the high school where he taught in Petaluma for 13 years. Ram Goli, a senior accustomed to AP classes and the honors track, decided to take a class in the school's new makerspace called 3D MAKE. Ram recalls, "Being an AP student I felt that on the first day of class I would excel." But he soon realized, "that wasn't the case." Their first assignment was to build a freestanding structure they could use to protect themselves from a rainstorm for 24 hours. As his classmates drew up plans, collected materials and got to work, it dawned on the valedictorian that he had no actual skills to contribute to the work at hand. That, and he had just managed to cut his finger with an X-acto knife.

In all of his honors classes he had never been asked to work as part of a team, to plan and execute a project. He'd never been asked to design something or to build it. As he watched his classmates he realized that his schooling was in many ways deficient, devoid of collaborative experiences that produced something of immediate value for the the community. His graduation speech was an impassioned plea for educators to incorporate more real-world experiences into their classes. To provide opportunities to learn from failure in a way he felt was impossible in his AP classes. Ram wanted to increase the opportunities for students to connect to world beyond the school walls and to experience something real. Chuck took the valedictorian's message to heart.

For Jessica Progulske, the Work Based Learning Coordinator at SCOE, the challenge of bringing more authentic learning experiences to more students emerged from her first teaching job in a Los Angeles continuation high school, where she taught all subjects to her 9-12th grade students. "It was the perfect spot for thinking about our underserved kids," she recalls. Fresh from a degree in cultural anthropology (a major she and Chuck share) and the eldest in her family, Jessica had a soft spot for adolescents and was eager to advance social justice and take on the profound responsibility of working with marginalized youth. In Sonoma, Jessica worked as an English, science and math teacher at Windsor High School and started the Phoenix Intervention Academy, a pathway for students who traditionally struggled in school. "It was imperative that we focused on both cognitive engagement and the social and emotional aspects of learning." Jessica explains. "We constantly thought about how to connect students to work that mattered to them."

Windsor High School is unique in Sonoma County, as one of the few schools to use a cohort teaching model. Trios of teachers share 90 students and have autonomy over their schedule. Whole teams often spend time off site engaged in work in the surrounding community. When Jessica joined SCOE, it was eye-opening to discover that other county schools were not set up for the cross-disciplinary integration and community connections she was accustomed to. Her work in helping underserved youth see opportunities for themselves in the professional world underscored the importance of providing students with real-world experiences, experiences that seemed to be few and far between for most of the county's students. Similar to schools across the country, Sonoma schools offer traditional college track classes—Advanced Placement and honors courses that cover A through G requirements for entrance into California's four year universities – and Career Technical Education (CTE) programs geared towards training for a particular occupation post high school or a postsecondary trade program. However, there is often little overlap between the two programs. Students tend to identify with one track or the other and rarely experience the "other side." This separation can leave students trapped on either side of an artificial divide. Many students in the academic streams feel the work they are doing is irrelevant to their lives and serves only as necessary hoops for a better life later on, while students in the CTE programs find that if they decide to pursue their chosen program at a university, their high school courses may not meet the A-G requirements for direct admission and they need additional courses to be eligible to apply.

Spurred by the ongoing conversations about the CTE/college track divide, Stephen Jackson, Director of Student Support Services at SCOE convened focus groups of teachers, administrators, and district office personnel from around the county to discuss how to bring about systematic instructional shifts to prepare their students for life after high school. From these conversations the SCOE team identified four key focus areas: develop supports for integrated project-based learning (PBL), use work-based learning as an instructional strategy, support the postsecondary transition process to college, and enhance wrap-around services to support all three initiatives.

The SCOE team explored a new Linked Learning program that focused on uniting rigorous core academic classes with career technical education and work-based learning opportunities such as internships, job shadows, or apprenticeships. The program advocates for the creation of distinct high school course pathways that provide students with learning experiences more connected to the professions they may choose after school, while still remaining eligible for applying directly to a four-year college after high school. The philosophy underlying the Linked Learning pathways is that "students work harder and dream bigger if education is relevant to them."[3] The program goal is to increase the number of students, particularly low-income or disadvantaged students, who graduate ready for college and with the skills needed to thrive in the adult workforce. In 2013 SCOE applied for a California Career Pathways Trust grant to support expanding career pathway programs in Sonoma County high schools and community colleges inspired by the Linked Learning model. One hundred and fifty two businesses wrote letters of support for the initiative.

In May 2014 they were awarded the grant[4] and Stephen, Chuck and Jessica went to work. What resources would the team need to put in place to support shifts in teacher identity as teachers adopted a more project-based learning pedagogy? What structures would help bridge the divide between schools and the local businesses? To begin the transition towards a more integrated system of school and community for Santa Rosa students, the team expanded existing professional development offerings such as their C3 Project-Based Learning and Summer Institutes, and created a series of teacher summer externship experiences with community partners, and two yearlong fellowships – one for principals and one for teachers ready to take their projects to the next level. Keenly aware of the mindset, pedagogical, and structural barriers they faced, the SCOE team dedicated themselves to helping teachers navigate the new expectations to find success for themselves and their students.

Dan & Katie: Connections Across Disciplines

In response to the new grant initiative, schools across Sonoma County began the process of figuring out how to modify their master schedules to integrate core academic courses with their CTE classes in order to create coherent Linked Learning pathways for their students. Different schools created different pathway structures, each with varying degrees of cohesiveness. In some schools, such as Windsor High School, the design of the school teaching structure allowed every student to choose a pathway and move together through high school in a cohort. In other schools the pathways are threads of course options that students can opt into during their high school career.

At Elsie Allen High School, Dan and Katie were encouraged by the administration to pair Katie's academic world history class with Dan's public safety classes, part of the Career Technical Education (CTE) program at Elsie Allen. Not only did Dan and Katie have to find a way to integrate the content of their two radically different courses together, but they also had to use a project-based approach to connect their students to the community and the world of adult work, not an easy task for any teacher, let alone a first-year teacher.

Recognizing the immense challenge facing teachers, the SCOE team designed week-long summer externship experiences with local businesses and community agencies to help teachers get a sense of what different occupations look like in the day-to-day of adult work.

Katie recalls one of her early planning meetings with Dan when he told her they were going to spend a week exploring homelessness.

> I started out being resistant to the homelessness topic, not because I don't care about it. Obviously it's a very big issue in Santa Rosa. But, when we look back at history, and at world history specifically, I wasn't finding a link that I felt confident in bringing back to my classroom. Going through the externship at the time, I really didn't know where we were going to go with it, or what the goal was going to be. We were connected to the police chief. He wanted to give us a way where we could see all these different agencies in Santa Rosa and how they work together with police officers. He believed that the homelessness issue was going to give us the most well-rounded view of how all those agencies work together. And it really

did. We went to the water board, we went to the fire department, and of course we talked with police officers. We did a lot of work with Catholic Charities.

Throughout their experiences Dan and Katie looked for ideas they could bring into their respective classrooms. "As we started studying and looking at different avenues [for collaboration], we realized that we could expand it, not just about homelessness, but about being involved in your community and your community's needs." Katie and Dan decided to have students explore the unintended consequences of political decisions. They designed a project where students explored what happens to communities when they were forced into small spaces, specifically the encampments that occurred during the industrial revolution.

Katie launched the project in her classroom by exploring how different community agencies work together to help the homeless. "One of my big takeaways was bringing authentic documents into our classrooms that students got to use. We were given a rubric from the Catholic Charities that they use to place homeless people into permanent housing. It's called the Host Program."

Katie gave her students anonymous bios of real homeless people in Sonoma county and asked them to use the rubric to determine who would be housed. The students worked in groups to determine who was the most at risk.

> Students had to make this really hard decision that people in a real job have to make every day. It's not who do you want to place, or who's friendly with you, or who do you think will be the most successful. The criteria that they have to use is based on who is the most at risk and needs this housing most immediately.

The authenticity was ratcheted pretty quickly for [students] when they realized, "Oh! These are life and death choices we're making."

The C3 Project-Based Learning Institute: A Day of Feedback

To support teacher teams in developing cross-disciplinary projects, Chuck and Jessica run a yearly three-day PBL institute where teachers have time to brainstorm, discuss, and plan projects that would ordinarily be impossible to create within the time allotted for teacher collaboration at their respective schools.

The final day of the C3 Project Based Learning Institute for Sonoma County teachers took place on a cold overcast February day at 180 Studios, a cavernous warehouse community makerspace in southwest Santa Rosa. Teachers, dressed in warm jackets and scarves, poured themselves coffee and mingled amidst the lathes and bandsaws. There were hopeful predictions that the day would be dryer than the previous two workshop days back in January. A massive industrial heater suspended high over the workspace rumbled continuously. Chuck and Jessica gave a one-minute warning to refill coffee cups and then welcomed the seven teacher teams from K-12 schools across the county back for a full day of feedback on their emerging project plans.

Connecting Teachers to Teachers

When teachers first engage in thinking about projects, their ideas are often limited in scope to in-class activities that can easily remain isolated from the real world. Given time to dream and come up with ideas with colleagues, the teaching teams were ready to go big. One team designed a project to explore the effects of mental illness on their community in order to raise public awareness about the issue. Riffing on Trump's plans for a US-Mexico border wall, a team of teachers from Cloverdale High School planned to have students create an art installation in the shape of a wall for downtown Cloverdale showcasing students' written and visual work exploring the guiding questions, "What is truth?" and "What are barriers to truth and how can we overcome them?" An English and art teacher were collaborating to have students create and publish their own books. A middle school science teacher wanted to explore local river ecosystems and monitor the health of their nearby stream. And a teacher of a special day program that had started its own in-school coffee shop had discovered that their profits had dropped. The students wanted to figure out why, and what they could do to boost sales.

Chuck and Jessica set the stage for the day by launching with a round of peer feedback. Teams pitched their projects and the other teachers in the room provided ideas and resources. As facilitators, Chuck and Jessica provided helpful sentence starters such as, "Have you thought about...", "You could read/watch/visit..." "It would be awesome if...". The feedback came fast and furious. Teachers built off of each other's suggestions, drawing from a wide range of curriculum, community, and pop culture resources.

> "You could introduce Plato's cave analogy of truth."
> "Or explore pop culture references to walls, like Pink Floyd."
> "Did you think about using a design thinking process to teach that?"
> "Have you reached out to local community agencies for mental health experts?"

The ease with which teachers from different disciplines shared ideas across the proposed projects likely stemmed from the real world nature of the projects themselves. They were relatable and part of the fabric of our culture. Each project felt like work worth doing. At the first break the room was buzzing with energy and excitement.

During the feedback session Chuck and Jessica asked probing questions, "Is that something students want to solve?" "Hold a student in your mind. How would that student respond to this idea?" to bring awareness back to their core goal – that students engage in work that is meaningful to themselves and others. Throughout the process, Chuck and Jessica were a synergistic marvel, facilitating the discussion with care and thoughtfulness. Jessica later confided that they work together so frequently that teachers often refer to them affectionately as Chuckica.

For many of the teachers the C3 PBL Institute provides their first exposure to planning a project together. "Most of the teachers in attendance come from traditional schools with minimal time for teacher collaboration," Jessica points out. "We try to honor the need for teachers to have flexible team planning time." The three-day Institute is composed of optional breakout sessions around project design and community connections. Teachers have the opportunity to examine past projects, brainstorm project questions and learning goals, align curriculum with industry skills, and explore how to bridge the divide between their classroom and the surrounding community more effectively for their students. For the final day of the Institute, the focus is squarely on the latter goal. Chuck explained:

> Today is all about feedback and iteration. We are requiring that [teachers] get some feedback from students, that they get some feedback from community or industry partners, and that they get some feedback from each other in the

form of a project tuning[5] with their colleagues. When we do professional development work with teachers around projects, we talk about finding the sweet spot between desirability, viability, and feasibility. We want the projects to be highly desirable to students. We think higher levels of student engagement really make for better learning. It's more fun for teachers too.

It is also important to get feedback from colleagues as they are often key to bringing a project idea back to Earth. "We fall in love with our project ideas a little bit." Chuck confesses. When the traditional barriers found in schools that separate academic subjects from real-world work are removed the new possibilities are enticing. 'Wow, this is such a cool project, I'm going to build this out, and I'm thinking of 400 really amazing things I can do with kids, then – oh darn. I was supposed to be teaching biology. I forgot about that part." Feedback from other educators is crucial for determining if a project is viable and will provide students with the skills and tools they need for future success.

With regard to feasibility, Chuck feels that it is "really valuable to have input from industry partners to create the most engaging possible transformative learning experiences for students." In his experience, teachers often come up with amazing ideas only to get stuck on logistics or hung up on details that could be solved with access to occupational expertise. When would the average teacher come across the authentic intake documents for homeless people? This is where the feedback from professionals can be most valuable. "The community has been incredibly generous, but it does require that we ask." They can provide access to resources or information that can make or break a project. Jessica agrees.

C3 is designed to help teachers overcome the structural barriers inherent in their current school environments. Many of the teachers here don't share the same students, don't have common planning time, and don't have access at their schools to PBL expertise. Everything that the literature says you need to successfully implement PBL is missing. Our obligation is to help teachers maneuver around these systemic challenges.

Connecting Teachers to Students

After break, teacher teams moved to one of the individual rooms that surround the warehouse for another round of feedback on their projects from a student perspective. Surrounded by warm panelling and nestled on mid-century couches and space-age rolling chairs, teachers met with seniors, Colleen, Victor, Daniel, Merlyn, and Lexie, and junior Peyton, from the Nueva School of Performing Arts, a career pathway option at nearby Windsor High School.

The nervously eager students were primed with the "Six A's" of project based learning, from Adria Steinberg's *Real Learning, Real Work,* to help guide their discussions with the teacher teams. The Six A's are a useful checklist to ensure that a project has all the ingredients to be a rich and meaningful learning experience, and include: authenticity, academic rigor, applied learning, active exploration, adult relationships, and assessment.

Christi, a photography teacher at Cloverdale introduced their "What is Truth?" project idea. "Our project is an interdisciplinary project between English, history, and art students." Wendy, an English and world history teacher, continued. "We're going to ask [students] in different classes to look at the idea of truth, and how we examine

Wendy Connor, Cloverdale High School, with colleagues.

Inspiration, Not Replication

truth and what changes our perception of truth. We want our students to explore the idea of how they know what truth is." The team's choice of topic was inspired by Kellyanne Conway's use of the term "alternative facts" to describe stories reported in the media. Wendy continues, "and the need we see in our kids to really evaluate evidence." The Cloverdale team explained how they plan to have English students create written work and meld it with student work from art and photography classes to create panels to build an art installation 'wall' to be exhibited in downtown Cloverdale.

Cloverdale High School is a traditional school complete with fifty-minute periods, teacher break rooms, a school mascot, and segregated disciplines. Christi, Joe, and Wendy rarely have the same students in their classes, so they have developed strategies to have students from one class be use and interpret the work of students in another class. The plan they drew up called for Wendy's English students to provide written work that would be incorporated and interpreted by Christi's photography students, and finally molded into art pieces to be displayed on the wall, which, in keeping with the general spirit of real-world collaborations, would be constructed by yet another group of students.

After hearing about their project idea and the constraints they were working within, Daniel took a deep breath. "Don't give students two days to think about this question, or even a week. For a question this big they need time to have their ideas change and evolve, they need class structures to help them discuss their ideas and interact with each other."

Peyton cautioned against overly controlling the student art work, explaining that if the teachers wanted students to take ownership of the process they had to allow students to have some creative control, especially if they were working with another student's text. The students also shared classroom strategies that they felt helped them think through complex ideas, such as plenty of time for small group discussions, reading about different perspectives on the topic, and having enough time so that as their understanding evolved they could change their minds about what they wanted to present. The teachers nodded while taking notes.

Later, the students reflected on the opportunity to provide feedback to the teachers. "It was a really incredible experience. I almost can't explain it. It was empowering!" said Victor, another senior from Windsor. The students unanimously felt like they were able to help design a project that they would want to do. They felt like their voices mattered and their expertise was valued by others in their community.

Connecting Teachers to the Community

As Christi, Joe, and Wendy processed the student feedback together, Chuck and Jessica welcomed newly arriving community members for another round of feedback, this time from a professional perspective. After the last two days together in January, Chuck explains, "We scrambled to find the ideal community and industry partners to match with the project ideas teachers had developed so far."

For the Cloverdale team, Stephen had contacted reporters Kerry Benefield and Robert Digitale from the *Press Democrat*, the local Santa Rosa newspaper. The pair listened intently as the teachers outlined their project idea.

Joe explained how he wants students to think critically about what they're told. "It's not just sitting with your folks at the dinner table and them telling you how it is."

Wendy agreed. "Seeking the truth is complex, and takes time, but it's worth it."

The discussion that followed touched on different types of writing that the students could produce during the course of the project, from personal narratives about what students believe to be true, to investigative journalism essays on topics they care about. As with any topic of such philosophical weight, eventually the very nature of truth was questioned. Kerry and Robert shared some of their concerns about the slippery nature of truth in journalism. How much of the truth is in the eye of the beholder? How many perspectives need to be sought out for a reporter to feel certain of the facts?

Kerry explained how seeking truth in journalism is an iterative process. She starts with just the kernel of a story, the bare essential facts she feels most confident about, and then poses a question for her readers about the perceived truth that the facts seem to point to. This usually sparks an influx of new information and threads to pull on. "Did you talk to this person?" "Did you get that person's perspective?" She uses the new leads to help guide further exploration and to flesh out her stories with additional supporting evidence.

This explanation led to a new topic of conversation for the group. Which information sources are valued more than others, and why? And which facts are left out? What does that tell us about the truth being presented? And what role do reporters play as interpreters of evidence and how does that impact the process of uncovering the truth? Kerry added, "or you could explore how the language we use impacts understanding. The weight of language and what people bring to it." For Christi, Joe, and Wendy the possible authentic learning objectives for their project had just expanded a hundredfold.

Joe Dobbins, Cloverdale High School

Inspiration, Not Replication

The Cloverdale team's next community expert was local sculptor and craftsman, Bruce Johnson. Bruce builds breathtaking sculptures out of metal and massive trunks of trees. His pieces are a study in mass and scale, often playing with themes of imbalance—a nod to the vanishing ecosystems of his favorite material, the majestic redwood. Bruce's feedback focused on the actual construction of the wall art installation. How could the materials used to build the wall also convey the students' understanding of truth? He shared work by UCSD Cross Border Initiative Founder Teddy Cruz who challenged artists to rethink the Mexico-US wall and received ideas as diverse as building it out of solar panels (to, you know, actually make it useful), incorporating doors and windows to deliberately undermine its isolationist message by suggesting that people on the two sides should frequently visit each other, and building sections out of volleyball net to inspire impromptu international sporting events. In addition to opening the creative floodgates on ways the wall could be constructed, Bruce also suggested that the teachers contact local building contractors in their area to become the contractor's downstream waste plan for upcoming projects. He had just picked up 50 feet of leftover sheet metal from a nearby project that would have been scrapped at an added cost to the builder. The teachers would be doing the contractors a favor and the students would get free construction materials.

C3 Impact

Back together at the end of the day, the teams shared their takeaways. Joe mentioned Kerry and Robert. "We met with journalists from the local paper, the Press Democrat. That gave us a path for how to move forward."

Wendy spoke about Bruce. "The artist gave us ideas for how to collect materials for the work, things I never thought about." She lauded students' feedback. "The piece that was important to the students is making sure that we craft the project so that they have a little bit of structure but not so much that it squelches their creativity."

All the teacher teams' stories were similar. The middle school teacher exploring watershed ecosystems had been put in touch with a local ecologist who loved to put on rubber boots and share her enthusiastic expertise of healthy rivers with students. The team exploring mental health was now connected to a psychologist who worked at the local prison – a connection guaranteed to keep their students riveted. Illustrators and authors were lined up to support students in becoming published authors, and owners of the local community coffee shop offered to donate beans to the school coffee business and train students in the art of the perfect pour over.

"I wish all our staff meetings were like that!" Wendy exclaimed as the teachers debriefed in the main hall. They were excited, brimming with new ideas, and clearly exhausted. Chuck and Jessica thanked everyone for their passion and enthusiasm to create more meaningful learning experiences for students. Now it was time to celebrate, Sonoma style, with wine and cheese.

Chuck confided:

> It's a magical day for me, a little bit, this day three of the Institute, when we bring the community and industry partners together with teachers. Teachers walk in, in the morning with a rough idea of a project, and they generally feel pretty good about it. By the end of the day those projects have pivoted 180 degrees. They're doing something totally different, and they feel even better about it.

Teacher Externship

In order to design more authentic learning experiences for students teachers have to unlearn years of schooling and embrace new project based educator identities. To support this process, Chuck and Jessica set up immersive summer externship experiences.

"They have an opportunity to have a shared experience as part of a teacher externship. They get to experience what it's like to be an adult in a particular industry area and discover their standards in the wild, so to speak." Chuck continues, "And bring back authentic experiences for their students that are analogous to what adults are doing in the workplace."

Windsor High School: Discovering Standards in the Wild

At Windsor High School, students choose one of seven different pathways for their high school career: Advanced Placement Core, Arete Digital Media and Design Core, Axis STEM Core, The Humanities School of Communications, Nueva School of the Performing Arts (some of whose students provided feedback during the C3 PBL institute), Pre-Med Core, and Vineyard Academy. Each cohort of students participates in interdisciplinary projects designed by teacher teams of three that relate to their particular pathway theme. The Vineyard Academy students put on an annual chili cook-off that draws 15 fire departments and 15 local businesses. They also grow grapes on a nearby vineyard that are used to produce an old vine Zinfandel. Profits from the chili cook-off and wine sales fund classroom supplies like Macbooks and most recently, a bullet-nosed trailer for hauling catering and farm equipment.

Many of the teachers at Windsor High School have participated in one of the teacher externship experiences organized by Chuck and Jessica. The externship experiences take place across Santa Rosa. Teachers spend a week with community agencies, as Dan and Katie did with the police force learning about homelessness. Marie, the culinary instructor in the Vineyard Academy pathway at Windsor, spent a week with John Ash & Co, a local Inn and kitchen facility that serves as a hub for a hotel, a catering business, and a restaurant.

Kate Fitzgerald, a humanities teacher at Windsor and her engineering teaching partner Sean Vezino reflected on their externship experience at Keysight Technologies in Santa Rosa. "One week, one super intensive week with these really hyper professional engineers, who were amazing." Kate qualifies, "but they literally scheduled every moment. We had to ask to go to the bathroom." "Kind of like we do in school." Sean points out.

Keysight Technologies, a spinoff company from Hewlett Packard, sits on a sprawling acreage in the verdant hills east of Santa Rosa. The home to 3,000 employees is an expansive complex of laboratories, offices, fabrication warehouses, and production facilities focused on developing technologies of the future. A 20-foot-high wall covered in patents awaits visitors after they enter the building. The US headquarters oversees sites in ten different countries and more than 10,000 employees conducting research in the areas of software, heterogeneous computing systems, human-computer interaction, wireless technologies, photonics, imaging, and modeling.

"They had a really cool project for us, but we had to ask for the time to reflect on what it would look like in the classroom." Kate continues, "That week, working together and being put in an uncomfortable position really mirrored what our students would have to do."

The Keysight engineers created an externship experience where Kate and Sean and other participating teachers engaged in an authentic design process, prototyping and coding dog tracking devices. "That changed the way we planned. It really did, because now we had a language. That organized industry partner connection was super important in how we plan, and how we structure our projects, and how we look at what we want to do next."

Sean agreed, "The project that directly resulted from that was a six-week intensive, where we didn't even have individual classes. We just took [students] through this R&D process that we emulated off of the Keysight experience." The student project that emerged from using the design and prototyping process was impressive. Students redesigned public spaces in Windsor to make them more integral to the community, and then presented their ideas to the mayor of Windsor and the Parks and Recreation Director. Several student teams were also asked to present their prototypes at the town council meeting.

"It changed the way I teach English in this focus area," Kate says of their STEM pathway focus. "When I started I was trying to just plug in technology and engineering where I thought it would fit and it felt really unauthentic. I was struggling." The Keysight experience helped her realize:

> It has to be the the complete opposite. I have to find a way to embrace the technology and teach English through that. I was in charge of coding the little dog tracker, and what I realized was coding is just a language, and a language has grammar and structure. And there it was. It was like this awakening moment for me.

Right now we're doing a science fiction unit,

Student Projects Mirror the "Real World"

Keysight Business Process Analyst Jim Churchill oversees the weeklong summer teacher externship experience at Keysight and also visits schools to share his experiences with managing large international collaborations. His last visit with a student project team at Windsor High School came at an opportune time. The students in the Axis STEM core responsible for management of their semester project were having a team crisis. Productivity was dropping and student relationships, sorely needed for the success of the project, were deteriorating. Jim realized that the students were wrestling with the same issues that his engineering teams deal with on a regular basis.

> We're working with multiple teams of people, different personality types, different cultures, language barriers. You have to figure out how to work together to achieve one goal that everybody's working towards. And even if we're all in the same room together we might have different communication styles. If I'm working with you, you might interact better one on one and through conversation, and other people might like text messages, and others want to see an email.

Jim's experiences resonated with the kids—they realized that the challenges they faced working with classmates were inhibiting their ability to make progress on their project. With Jim's help they realized that they were going to have to learn new skills to communicate effectively if they wanted to get their prototypes done in time. They had been communicating *to* their classmates, instead of *with* their classmates. Success in their project was dependent on removing barriers even at the student-to-student level.

where I'm able to teach all of my literacy content standards, but through a lens that they embrace and enjoy. I can talk about the rhetoric of video games, or the thematic links between stories and science fiction. It allows me to do my English content, but embed the STEM focus area. It was all that summer institute.

Sean continues, "Now the English/history content, as much as it can, ends up being the topical driving force, and then we use the engineering skills to flesh out what they actually produce from it." When asked about their proudest moment during the project, Sean laughs, "I can't believe we did it. That's all projects. There's this dip in the middle of it and you're like, we're not going to survive!"

"Then we do," Kate adds, "and the kids learn, and they come back, and they're leaders."

Elsie Allen High School: Embracing Risk

There is a 9.1 year difference in lifespan of people living on the east side of Highway 101 and those living on the west side as it passes through Santa Rosa.[6] The life-expectancy divide maps onto economic disparities between the younger and more racially mixed population of the west, and the older more affluent and homogeneous populations of the east. The segregation of neighborhoods also results in de facto segregation of schools.

Elsie Allen High School in southwest Santa Rosa, where Katie Chesbro and her pathway partner Dan Bartholome teach, was unusually quiet. The 1600 students ordinarily crowding the common spaces between classes, were largely absent. It was the national Day Without an Immigrant and the predominantly Latino student population had stayed home to protest the Trump administration's immigration agenda. At the bell three girls sat down in Katie's history class. The rest of the desks sat empty.

Katie and Dan are in their second year of coplanning cross-disciplinary projects together. After their first externship experience in the homeless encampment, they signed up again, this time with the Santa Rosa Fire Department. According to Katie:

> [This year] we worked with the fire marshal, assistant fire marshal, plans examiner, the investigators, the inspectors. We were able to learn all about how fire inspection happens around Sonoma County. Not only pre-fire inspection, but also looking at photographs and evidence from fires that have happened and exploring how the fire marshal figures out how the fire started.

From the externship experience Dan realized that "it takes a special person to write and live the fire codes." He realized quickly that if he lectured to his students about them he was likely to "put them to sleep." Instead, he decided to take a risk and learn alongside his students. He brought in an inspector to assess his classroom for violations. "Ian walked in my room and said you can't do this, you can't do that, and can't do that, and the kids are in awe that I'm in violation." Dan smiles, "They were like—Wow! That's so cool!"

The students couldn't wait to use their newfound knowledge on other classrooms in the building. Visiting their prior teachers' classrooms they performed inspections throughout the middle school for the fire department. The student teams became fire code experts, writing up polished professional reports to present to the fire marshal and assistant fire marshal.

In Katie's class, students linked the fire theme to their

study of the industrial revolution. What role did safety play with all the new factories? They examined historical fires and their significance to the surrounding community. Using their newfound knowledge of fire codes, students pieced together what must have occurred and built models to explain their thinking. Katie explained that her students were able to show, "how if certain fire codes had been in place at the time, or if certain violations had not occurred how it would have affected the loss of life or loss of property." In a tragic turn of events, the Oakland Ghostship warehouse fire occurred during the course of their project, bringing home the real-world consequences of fires, the importance of fire inspections, and the deep impact fires can have on the community.

Elsie Allen is a traditional high school so Dan and Katie worked with their administrator to ensure that they could share a set of students. "We were also able to bring our coach, Anna, who's been extremely helpful." Katie continues, "We're able to get released time for us to work together."

Dan agrees, "The time and resources it takes to put one of these projects together…, I won't say it's astronomical, but it's pretty high. We need that extra time in the summer, we need that support we get from SCOE, we get from Anna, we get from Chuck."

Despite her initial reluctance to embark on cross-disciplinary project design during her first year of teaching, Katie explains her growing enthusiasm for co-designing projects for the Linked Learning program, "I started seeing how the students lit up when we brought in authentic documents, or when they were able to collaborate with the same classmates from one class to the other. They always talk about how it's a family. I noticed how powerful this program can really be."

Anna Koval, Sonoma County Office of Education

Inspiration, Not Replication

Continuing Coaching Support

Integrated career pathway coaches are one of the integral support structures for teachers who go through the C3 Project Based Learning Institute. They help teachers develop and carry out their project ideas even within the challenging structures of the more traditional county schools. Chuck feels that, "It's really important for teachers to have support after they've received some professional development so that they can have help in implementing what they've learned in their own context."

Asking teachers to overhaul the way they teach and to suddenly design projects and bring in community connections "can be a real challenge for teachers who are learning about things in sort of an idealized form." In our institutes and fellowships a lot of time is spent thinking about what could be. "This is what it would look like if conditions were perfect." But Chuck continues:

> They don't have perfect conditions. Few of them have the kinds of supports that the research says is necessary for these kinds of things to work, like students in common, common planning time, and release time to really dig into designing the best possible kind of experiences for their students. Coaching has been an essential part of the success of the program because coaches can serve as thinking partners for teachers in problem solving and making things happen. Coaches allow them to feel that they have support in situations that are often really trying for them.

Anna Koval, an integrated career pathway coach explains, "I work with [teachers] during their planning times, prep periods, collaboration times, and classes to enrich and deepen the work they want to do with their students."

Together with the teaching teams, Anna works to identify curricular goals and what experiences the teachers hope their students leave with. "Often it's a sense of confidence. So many of our students are from low socioeconomic backgrounds," and there are "a variety of personal challenges that they bring with them to campus." Which is why, for Anna, it is so inspiring when the students say, "I can see myself doing that job."

Anna smiles, "that's what we're doing this for."

They've Got Roots Here

When asked why businesses participate in the externship program, Jim responds, "From a technology standpoint, industry has to take some responsibility of partnering early on because this is our workforce of the future. Our company is aging out in another 10 or 15 years. When this generation retires where is the next generation of technologist engineers going to come from?"

"To be able to reach back now at the junior high level, high school level, plant those seeds, those sparks of excitement for future careers, ... it's just the thing that we have to do. If we don't, then industry is going to lose out."

"We want students that are growing up in this community to come back and work for us. They've got roots here, they've got family here. It's imperative to make sure there's an opportunity for them to do that."

The Student Perspective

Perhaps the most compelling evidence for the importance of connecting students to the adult world came from the students themselves. When asked to compare their more traditional elementary and middle school experiences to their project-based experiences at Windsor High School, the students at the C3 PBL Institute touched on the importance of doing work that matters to others, the motivating factor of authentic adult audiences, and the real world skills learned throughout the process.

In their latest project the Neuva team was commissioned by the school to redesign a number of classroom and public spaces. Project teams conducted empathy interviews with people who used the spaces on a regular basis, researched interior design techniques, talked to professionals in the field, and drew up plans for revisioning the spaces. Merlyn said:

> I never thought I would be interested in space design, and I still don't think it's something I would pursue, but it was awesome that it was tangible. It was really cool that it was something totally applicable, it wasn't—"Here, read this chapter and write a report on it or do a tri-fold." It was—"Talk to people, talk to your community, research the psychology of color and come up with a plan.

Victor, another senior at Windsor continues:

> We presented to a panel with industry professionals. The head of budgeting for Sonoma County, interior designers, teachers who would be using the space. That was really the nail in the coffin for authenticity. It felt real. When it's just a regular in-school project, it's

like, "Pretend we're going to do this." Well, okay, I can just do whatever I want because it's not real.

The industry panel was going to select one of the students' designs to implement. Once a design was chosen, students would have the opportunity to work with interior designers to redesign the communal space. Victor explains, "When there is a lot on the line and you are aware that it is a legitimate project you put more effort into it. You take pride in everything you do and the decisions you make."

The students also identified some challenges of project-based learning. Perhaps the most persistent challenge is that it is sometimes difficult for classmates to understand that the project is a real learning opportunity. It can feel unfamiliar and scary. Students have spent so long in traditional school situations it can take a while for them to recognize and value the real world experiences they're having.

When asked how using project-based learning and work-based learning opportunities earlier in the schooling process might affect students, Daniel hypothesized:

> I think it would produce more interest in their education. Because with elementary school and middle school, I was handed a textbook, I was told what pages to read and then what to take notes on, and then to turn in those notes, get a grade, pass my test, pass the class. And that class was going to help me to pass my classes in high school which were going to help me pass my classes in college. But to what extent would that actually help me? Not much. When you have a job or when you are working in a real life situation, you're not handed a textbook,

told to take notes on it, and then asked to solve a world crisis that way. You need to problem solve and you're supposed to work hands-on with other people with experience and expertise.

Victor agreed, and added that introducing project based learning earlier:

[W]ould allow students to have a different perspective on their education. If we're constantly giving elementary students a textbook to read, they're going to think that that's what education is about, when it's not. It's about expanding your horizons, your opportunities, and your perspectives. I think that by making this more hands-on for elementary students, we're changing their perspective at a young age so they don't get into that educational rut where they're just constantly having their heads down in a book. While that can be beneficial, it's not the only way people learn.

Merlyn jumped in:

It's also cool to see that there's not just one teacher trying their hardest to push a program, but that multiple teachers are going out into the community and bringing in professionals." [It's important] that students also learn how to make those connections and think for themselves, and then think in different ways. To be able to, in the future, work with the professionals that they were introduced to in school.

The students also touched on how exposure to adults in the community through projects allowed them to see themselves as having an increased level of social maturity. "If you treat someone like they're a kid, they're not going to go beyond that expectation." Daniel explained, "The students aren't kids anymore. They can think for themselves. Yes, we don't have as much experience as adults do, but unless adults give us that chance to gain that experience, we won't go past that expectation of being a child."

Overcoming Barriers

Driven by a relentless belief in the potential of all students to graduate ready to contribute to the community, and a confidence that together, teachers and students can explore connections to professions outside of school and do work that matters, the SCOE team and the teachers they work with are truly inspiring.

Organizing externship summer experiences for over 52 teachers to help them envision authentic projects that help students develop real work skills, carving out time through the C3 PBL Institute for teachers to connect to colleagues, students, and the community as they plan their projects, and having integrated career pathway coaches like Anna, Chuck, Jessica and the rest of the SCOE team to support the continuing work have created an impressive web of interconnected support structures for teachers across the county.

"Our goal is about getting more relevance into all classes." Chuck explains, "I think all students can benefit from more relevant learning experiences. All students hope one day to have a career. College is not the end goal."

If communities are built from the connections between individuals, the work in Sonoma is a step in the right direction. Each interaction between professionals and students, or the teachers who serve them, not only strengthens the community, but also presents an image for students of what their role could be outside of school. Each experience helps students develop a more expansive view of their own identity, one where anything is possible.

References and Resources

1   Tony Miller, "Partnering for Education Reform," U.S. Department of Education, accessed February 18, 2015, https://www.ed.gov/news/speeches/partnering-education-reform.

2   Gallup Student Poll, 2015, http://www.gallupstudentpoll.com/file/188036/2015%20Gallup%20Student%20Poll%20-%20Overall%20Report.pdf.

3   "Linked Learning Prepares Students to Graduate from High School Ready for College and with Skills to Thrive in the Workplace," The James Irvine Foundation, https://www.irvine.org/linked-learning.

4   "Funding Results, California Career Pathways Trust," California Department of Education, January 9, 2017, http://www.cde.ca.gov/fg/fo/r17/ccpt14result.asp.
5   "Tuning Protocol: Overview," National School Reform Faculty, https://www.nsrfharmony.org/system/files/protocols/tuning_0.pdf.

6   "A Portrait of Sonoma County," Measure of America of the Social Science Research Council, May 20, 2014, http://www.measureofamerica.org/sonoma/.

Jim Snyder,
Anderson Valley Junior Senior High School

Inspiration, Not Replication

A Quiet Revolution from the Fringes Inward
From Exhibition to Project-Based Learning

Kali Frederick
High Tech Middle Chula Vista

A dministrators at the local, state, and national levels frequently impose changes on schools from the top down. They impose new requirements that filter down to the teachers to institute in their classrooms; initiatives in this mode are often met with resentment from teachers because they have little to no say in identifying the problem to be solved, generating possible solutions, and deciding whether and how the new requirements are implemented. Teacher resistance can block bad ideas but also prevent desirable change. The alternative approach—engaging teachers from the beginning in designing and making changes that proceed from the ground up—is rare.

Anderson Valley Junior-Senior High School is in the midst of a quiet, grassroots revolution that is coming from a small group of teachers. Although these teachers and their classrooms are located at the fringes of the school, they aspire to change its core. These teachers and staff—Jim Snyder, Donna Pierson-Pugh, Mitch Mendosa, David

Ballantine, and Kim Jenderseck—are quietly inspiring a new set of expectations of how school operates and leading by example. Donna, the Grant Administrator for Anderson Valley schools, is a petite woman with sharp silver hair that frames her face. She is enthusiastic about the school and the community and is quick to identify who on campus could best respond to seemingly any question. With an easy going smile and contagious laughter, she summed up the culture of this school in one goal: "We are refugees from the suburbs and urban areas, looking to recreate the experiences that those places had to offer but in a rural setting. We are trying to avoid being called 'boonies.'"

Anderson Valley High School is located in the tiny town of Boonville, California, and, as Donna alluded to during a conversation with this author, the school beautifully balances its rural location and culture with a strong desire to give these students an engaging learning environment that prepares them for any setting, rural or not. These teachers are actively seeking to promote project-based learning (PBL) practices at their school because they want to increase student engagement and the quality of student work at their school. Enrollment at the school is declining, as Jim Synder observes, more and more families are sending their children to schools in the nearby cities with the perception that "bigger schools have more opportunities and facilities."

When you first meet Jim, you can't help but notice the energetic slight bounce in his step as he shows off the middle and high school campus. He starts our tour of the campus by showcasing the agricultural program for the high school. East of the school's entrance are three geodesic-domed buildings, connected in the center and the windows clouded by age. Leading to the domes is an aged wooden fence and walkway lined with vines, mirroring the vineyards that surround this rural community. Two rows of elderly apple trees are covered with moss. Two large greenhouses frame the small orchard and in the near distance, a rooster crows.

The rest of the school is a typical 1950s design: elderly blue checkered patterned curtains adorn the windows and wooden cabinets and chalkboards line the walls in each classroom. This rural environment is both beneficial and challenging to the school staff. However, the valley is also home to wealthy patrons from the wine and tech industry who give grants and raise funds for the school, making it possible to acquire sophisticated equipment for its science and vocational classes. The Career Technical Education (CTE) classrooms—auto shop, woodworking, music production, welding—are on the fringes, while the traditionally academic classes, such as English, math, history and science, are connected via two distinct hallways at the center of the campus. The six middle school classrooms are arrayed along one hallway, the six high school classrooms along the other. Three satellite structures that host the woodshop, music and audio classroom, and lunchroom surround the main building.

The spacious school grounds host 230 students for grades seven to twelve and 20 faculty members. The student body is 75% Hispanic or Latino, 24.1% White, and 0.4% Black or African American. English Learners are 19% of the student body and 82.3% of students are considered socioeconomically disadvantaged.[1] Some students come from families that have been in the area for three or more generations. Approximately half of the faculty members have been at the school for more than ten years and approximately half have taught at this school for less than four years. The outer buildings, where the CTE classes are held, are where PBL is developing, and are at the heart of the change—the teachers in these outer buildings hope to spread their practices and ideals into the central building.

Projects Already in Practice: A Culture to Build From

The school's CTE classes are inherently designed to support student projects. The classes focus on building technical skills. Typically, students work on a project that requires a final, real-world product for a few weeks before moving on to another product. In woodworking, for example, advanced students were working on dovetail joints and created traditional Japanese toolboxes. In a video production class, students created independent films that were shown school-wide during a 20 minute advisory period. In addition to woodworking (David and Jim prefer the term "industrial design") and video production, classes range from auto repair, culinary arts, and audio technology, to an agricultural program that utilizes the vast space and greenhouses found on school property. Beth Swehla, a 26-year veteran teacher, manages the agricultural program. Students plant seedlings, manage chickens and goats, and maintain the orchard. The produce and livestock are sold at a county fair that is hosted by the Future Farmers of America (FFA) in Boonville.

Within the traditionally academic classes, there is a required senior project that has been spearheaded for over 20 years by the lead English teacher, Kim Campbell. David spoke highly of this project because of the independence it allows students and the real-world process it walks students through. He summarized the project as follows:

> Students decide on a project, write a detailed proposal, and then execute it with a mentor to provide guidance. After completion, we spend two days watching as the students do a juried presentation for three judges, an array of community members, family and other students. It is a rite of passage for our seniors.

Projects and project-based learning are for the most part isolated to these particular classes. More than half of the student body takes CTE classes and is exposed to projects, but this group of teachers aims to introduce this type of hands-on learning into more classes .

One student in the audio technology class stayed after school to work on his latest recording for a friend. As he finalized the beats for a track, Ben, a senior, reflected on how he wished other classes were similar to music production. He found that when assignments and projects included building or creating products along with intellectual pursuits, he believed that he learned more and felt far more engaged. He lamented that other classes were just not interesting. "Because we live out here in the country, it makes sense to do projects that make us think and build. We are all used to working on farms and grew up with building. Why shouldn't our classes be the same?" Ben took Jim's music production class his junior year and it has changed the course of his future. He now makes music for local musicians and envisions himself going to college to study the music business.

Ben felt that the audio technology class challenged him in a way that other classes did not and felt more relevant to his interests and passions. This deeper personal connection is common in successful projects: when asked about the work they are most proud of at their school, faculty members reflect fondly on the project Mitch created—*The Voices from the Valley: Stories of Anderson Valley Elders Collected by Anderson Valley Youth*.

Engaging Students: The Birth of a Project

When he first started teaching, Mitch immediately recognized students' disengagement from traditional academics. He found one way to get them excited was through simulations—activities in which students

Mitch Mendosa,
Anderson Valley Junior Senior High School

Inspiration, Not Replication

conduct research and then participate in a model activity of what they are learning. The summer of 1989, he taught an English class for the summer school program for high school students who needed to catch up on credits. The students were bored and angry, and he quickly recognized that classroom management was going to be an issue. On a whim, he decided to bring in tape recording equipment. Originally, his idea was to have them work independently to record and transcribe a story from a family or community elder. Among other advantages, he figured that students wearing headphones wouldn't be so disruptive. After the first day, he saw how focused the students were when transcribing their families' stories and how excited they were to share their stories with their classmates. Attendance was high and students were engaged. He took it further and had the students design a cover, make copies of the stories and put them together in a stapled packet. They titled the stories "An Oral History of Anderson Valley."

Each year after, Mitch found a way to incorporate this project in various grades (seven to twelve) and to include other teachers in the process. Between 1998 and 2007, the project, known as *Voices of the Valley*, became a separate English class, focused entirely on publishing these books annually (Volumes I and II took two years to complete and publish, the subsequent volumes were completed in one year). He reflected that the personal nature of the project and the published final book motivated students to create polished pieces of writing. They strengthened their writing skills and practiced grammar as classmates edited their work, following guidelines for good writing they learned in their English class. Each publication had a book signing event where the authors and the elders signed the book. According to Mitch, the signing was "well attended by the community."

While this project inspired admiration from colleagues

and community members, it was an anomaly. Other teachers continued to conduct their classes according to state curriculum and testing requirements. Although Mitch did this project with another English teacher, Kim Campbell, curriculum and grants made it challenging for him to maintain this momentum to collaborate with the teachers. He reflected that it took a lot of time to collaborate and that time was not always allotted within the school day for the purpose.

When the school received California Career Pathways Trust grants in 2015, to be used in 2016 to enhance their pathways programs and explore professional development opportunities, Donna identified Jim and his four co-workers to send to the Career Pathways PBL Leadership Academy at High Tech High in San Diego. They were already doing hands-on projects and were enthusiastic about learning techniques and practices that would increase student engagement and enhance the quality of student work. The opportunity turned out to be the spark for their revolution.

The Value of Making Student Learning Public

Jim, Mitch, David, Kim, and Donna attended the PBL Leadership Academy Fall Leadership Institute at HTH in October 2016. Within Anderson Valley, this group became known as "the PBL Team." HTH students struck them as articulate, confident, knowledgeable—similar to their own students—but Mitch noticed HTH students did not hesitate to engage adults in a conversation. In general, HTH classrooms seemed to them to be more like workshops. The PBL Team was inspired by the amount and quality of student work displayed in HTH schools, and they homed in on the value of making student learning public via classroom or even school-wide exhibitions and the semi-permanent curation of student work. Jim said he "realized we had some of these components, we are doing projects, but we were missing the exhibition piece, and the exhibition piece would let people see what we were doing."

While visiting HTH, Jim noted the focus on the public display of student work. This is intentional. As Rob Riordan, co-founder of HTH, explains,

> Exhibitions create models of products, project designs, and effort. Exhibitions generate positive peer pressure. They help generate community support, including interest from local businesses and agencies, particularly as they see and hear students talking about their work.

For these teachers, whose goals were to improve student engagement and quality of work, and inspire other teachers to join them in these goals, the idea of an exhibition of student learning seemed to provide a culminating event that could do just that. If students knew their work was going to be shared with a broader audience, would they become more invested in the project? If teachers saw what students created and heard students present their learning, would they be inspired to join the movement?

The four teachers and Donna decided that by an exhibition of student learning , they could get other teachers interested in exploring new ways of engaging students in their own classes. Mitch said he could start by showcasing his film class products in advisory.

The PBL Team returned to Anderson Valley aspiring to lead a PBL revolution, but they were careful about how they presented this aspiration to the staff. As Jim put it, "We didn't want to come back and throw all of this [PBL] at our staff. We needed to think of how to gently introduce it." Jim empathized with the other teachers and

Kim Jenderseck,
Anderson Valley Junior Senior High School

Inspiration, Not Replication

understood the problems in expecting too much change too quickly. Mitch took the first step by sharing student-films almost weekly to be shown in advisory period.

Team members recognized that in introducing PBL to their school they would need to tread softly. As with most California schools, Smarter Balanced tests and Common Core Curriculum demand attention and create stress for teachers. Regardless of how the administration tries to support teachers' creativity or autonomy, the pressure to comply and guarantee the success of their students on these tests can be overwhelming. The teachers at Anderson Valley reflected that the administration does not put absolute pressure on them to only "teach to the test" but in staff meetings and as the prepared for their accreditation assessment from the Western Association of Schools and Colleges (WASC) this year, they saw the statistics on how their school compares to other schools in the state and they personally feel the pressure to do more to increase scores. Because the Common Core standards are new, teachers feel they spend a lot of time just trying to figure out how to adjust their curriculum to the new framework, and what is anticipated to be assessed on the next round of standardized tests. Facilitating widespread acceptance of PBL techniques and strategies could be challenging; teachers will wonder how this will impact classrooms and student experiences. However as Mitch put it, "No administrator would squash an incredible project idea." Jim knows that that it takes a huge "leap of faith" to introduce exhibitions and PBL practices into the classroom with Common Core and standardized tests looming over their heads, yet he is optimistic that teachers will eventually see "you will get there without checking off the boxes of the curriculum."

Projects From Passions

Ideas for authentic projects grow naturally from students' interests, clubs, or extravurriculars—places where students already take on significant responsibility.

Bert is a student with a slight figure and soft voice and wears large beaded necklaces with crosses hanging from the center; he is an aspiring rapper. Donna explained that he started his own composting project on campus, a project that was not part of any class.

Bert was eating lunch when he was struck by the amount of food and trash discarded by peers. He said he had seen videos on social media about garbage in the Pacific Ocean and it got him thinking about how to minimize trash at their school. Donna overheard him talking about the issue with friends and asked what they thought they could do. Bert suggested a garbage "audit." They would go through the garbage and separate what was compostable from the trash. Acting on this idea, they found that 80% of what was thrown away was compostable.

The day they built the composting bins, eight friends showed up—one wanted to take on the idea as his senior project. Donna suggested making the project public through a community meeting to inspire others.

At the community meeting, Bert dumped garbage on the floor in two piles, one of trash and the other of compost. He then showcased a compost bin and elicited support from the student body to change their behavior. The community meeting was a culminating exhibition for Bert, but a project launch for the school. More students joined into the project and made Bert more passionate about the topic. Today, Bert's compost bin is strategically placed on campus and he plans to make more.

Introducing PBL and the Idea of Exhibition

The PBL Leadership Academy experience includes a two-day in-house professional development (PD) session facilitated by their HTH Team Mentor. Jim worked with Jeremy Manger, a teacher at High Tech Elementary North County and his team mentor, to collaboratively design the professional development experience to fit the needs of the teachers and school. Jim's team organized the first day of PD into four one-hour workshops and arranged for substitutes to cover on a rotation system so that all teachers could attend and work with him and HTH staff, and that each teacher would only miss one class period of their day. Before the PD sessions began Jim anticipated that "you will see a lot of people making these connections saying 'Oh, we are already doing a lot of these things in our classes,' but we are not connected to each other ... and we don't have a process for it."

Jim errs on the side of leading by example rather than bombarding the teachers with PBL specifics. Before each workshop throughout the day, Jim introduced his vision for the professional development series: to have other teachers experience the creative, inspiring activities and protocols that help teachers dream up engaging projects for their students and ultimately inspire these teachers to join him in a school exhibition of student work. The sessions were designed to maximize creativity and inspiration. Students were invited and included as participants in each hour-long session.

On the first day of the two-day visit, the PD sessions with HTH staff were short, interactive, and engaging. They began with participants reflecting on a memorable moment of significant learning they had in their lifetime. This could be anything they learned at any point in their life—the only requirements are that the moment truly be memorable, and that it represent deep, lasting learning. Camaraderie grew as students and staff alike shared personal stories from finding a musical passion because a girlfriend inspired a song to appreciating the fragility of life because of the loss of a friend in a car accident. Importantly, the students and staff realized that most of their memorable moments of significant learning moments did not happen at school; most were deeply emotional, and involved an important personal relationship and a sense of self-efficacy. The question for the PD participants became: How do we create these moments of deep, emotional, engaged learning for all of the students in our school?

Next, the students and staff were challenged to compete as teams to quickly generate a list of at least fifty things that students could make, build or do. Small teams of teachers and students could win the impromptu competition two ways: by being the first team to list fifty things, or by being the team with the longest list in five minutes of frenzied brainstorming. If resources, money and time were not barriers, what could students do? The lists quickly grew: robots, rockets, apps, theatrical performances, documentaries, photo galleries, original music, comic books, organic produce for farmers' markets, and much more. The groups needed to think beyond the typical academic assignments; after each teacher wrote "essay" or "math problems" on their list, they had to move on quickly, or they would lose the competition. They then labelled and categorized their ideas according to whether the product seemed feasible, deeply emotional, or like an epic moon-shot for them and their students. Many realized that the pressures of school led them to make curricular choices according to feasibility, not necessarily potential for impact. However, in discussion they emphasized where these new final products would live and who would benefit from the project or learning experience. It was easy to grasp the concept and to become inspired by the mix of teachers and students sitting around a table, dreaming big.

Teachers reflected afterwards on student presence and student voice as critical to the process. During one session, a student reflected on how productive discussion groups of three were instead of two or four because "you can't hide in a group of three." And then she proceeded to explain what happens in a group of four or two. A teacher quickly responded, "I never thought of it that way, I always put kids in groups of four because of table arrangement. Next time I won't!" This "ah-ha" moment was striking because of the simplicity of the suggestion and the courage of the student to push back against the teacher's initial idea. Upon further reflection, one teacher mentioned that they had not seen "students as involved in a conversation around school before." This would prove to be an important observation that came up again after the next day's PD session.

First-Year Inspiration

Being a first-year teacher is hard no matter where you teach. One often feels like an isolated survivor of a shipwreck, drifting aimlessly and trying to stay alive. First-year Spanish teacher Adrian Moldonado was one of four teachers who approached Jim after the PD session to express interest in having more time for collaboration. Adrian spoke enthusiastically about his position and said he was excited about this PD opportunity because he could use all the help and ideas he could get.

During the PD session, Adrian expressed a desire to learn from other teachers how to incorporate and assess group activities into his class routines. As he said, "Group work is a great way to learn languages." However, his past experience with group work and class projects suggested that there is a "lack of effort in these projects. Students

Adrian Moldonado,
Anderson Valley Junior Senior High School

Inspiration, Not Replication

tried to get away with the bare minimum." As a reaction to this behavior, he planned an open-ended individual project. Students could choose any topic they wanted, research it, and present it in Spanish to the class in a five-minute slideshow. He believes the open-ended project has allowed for the motivated students to go above and beyond. However, he is frustrated because there are still some students who are not engaged; he saw the exact behavior he wanted to avoid repeated in this project. Quarterly student reflections about the class brought up interesting results that will help Adrian improve it for next time. Responses to the question "When the teacher pushes me do I step up?" the students Adrian was concerned about said they don't really try. In response to the question, "Do you feel comfortable in the class?" the same students reflected that they were stressed out. Adrian was seeking ways to change these feelings on this project and future projects.

He was so inspired by the hour-long activity and discussion that he asked to be part of the next day's session and attended the after-school debrief meeting the PBL Team had planned for themselves. He became an active participant in all of the activities and volunteered to be put in the truly vulnerable position of having a project he was doing with students critiqued, in public, by a group of students and teachers in a "project tuning protocol." During the project tuning, a student participant suggested that Adrian allow the presenters to invite someone to their presentation. Exhibiting the project to an audience that she cared about was a pivotal moment for this student. She mentioned that when she was able to invite someone to one of her presentations, "It made the work feel more important and I put more effort into the information I included and the visuals I used." In most traditional classrooms, the teacher is the only audience and critic for student work. This can make students feel as though the work doesn't have a real purpose or matter in their own lives. This feeling often leads to the perennial questions: Why are we doing this? When will I ever need to know this? Showcasing student work in front of an authentic audience helps students understand why they are doing it: it is for an event or someone else's benefit. After the project tuning, Adrian mulled over the idea of having students choose an audience that best fit their presentation topic. He was also eager to continue the conversation after school with the PBL Team.

The PBL Team and two mentors met at the end of the day to reflect on how the PD sessions went and to discuss how best to proceed. Now that the teachers had a taste of generating ideas for projects and seemed to be inspired by the idea of collaborating and working on parallel projects, what could they do next to harness the energy? They agreed that they needed to have an event—an exhibition of student learning to let other teachers see, first hand, the final product of a project and hear from students about the learning that went into the project.

As a group they decided to try to do three exhibitions by the end of the year. The first exhibition would be by just the core group of teachers who were at this meeting and would be held on April 3. The second exhibition would be in May and the final at the end of school in June. This would encourage teachers who came to see the exhibition to participate in the next one. The group hypothesized that if they could generate momentum for three in one semester, exhibitions might become routine in the following school year.

The First Exhibition: Creation Station

The flurry of activity before an exhibition can be overwhelming, stressful, and exciting. Students and teachers run around trying to make the space and the products presentable. The pressure of an audience can make students (and teachers) second guess their work. The first exhibition for the PBL Team, the "Creation Station," was held on April 3, 2017. Jim reported that the energy level was high and enthusiasm increased as students prepared for visitors. Mitch had his video students set up stations at all of the computers to highlight techniques they had learned and films they had created. Mitch related that:

> An unexpected moment came when we all stood back and looked at the room before guests arrived. In addition to the four stations, we had set up all the computers with student projects looped. After this was set up, a few of us stood back and uttered remarks like, 'Whoa, that looks good.' One of the students commented on the fact that it's hard to see the scope of the quantity and quality of what the class has produced thus far until the videos are played simultaneously.

Even though these students share videos in advisory on an almost weekly basis, the exhibition hosted all of their work at the same time and the students were impressed by how much they had learned and accomplished in class. This realization is an important consequence of exhibition: students and teachers need these moments when they are allowed to stop and celebrate their learning. Exhibitions inspire teachers and students to try harder.

Various classes exhibited their products. Kim's seventh grade science class displayed scientific method posters to showcase the diverse experiments students had designed and conducted. Robots designed by Jim's STEM class were another feature. His space science program class exhibited a weather balloon they had designed, launched, and tracked. Audio and film recording techniques used in student film projects took over the computers in the audio/video tech room. The Auto Shop students demonstrated how they troubleshoot a struggling car. Students showcased mallets and 3D printed objects in a display case, and staged a nearby demonstration of how a 3D printer works. All the students involved in the projects were on hand to present their work to the 40 community members who attended the event.

Jim invited a friend from the community who homeschools her children. In turn, she brought with her a few other homeschooling families. Upon leaving she turned to him and said, "If this is what you guys are doing, then I'm going to consider putting my kid back in this school." Knowing that the school district is experiencing declining enrollment, Jim was excited to hear this.

Jim also reported that in their WASC report (Western Association of Schools and Colleges—the accrediting agency) that was completed this year, the teachers agreed that they wanted more time to spend collaborating and PBL was a top priority. He felt hopeful that this exhibition was a start down the right track for their school.

Students' reflections after the exhibition demonstrated increased engagement. Jim's students collaborated on a Google document to share their experiences about what went well. Overall, the students (and the teachers) reported that the exhibition was well organized and that there were many interactive stations where audience members could learn from students. One student reflected that, "The students explaining the projects to the community made for positive interactions, also people came asking us questions about current and future projects." And another student said that one thing that went well was, "People I didn't know came up and asked me questions." Identifying conversations with unfamiliar community members as a highlight, students showed that having a chance to interact with community members can build their confidence in what they learned and make them feel like valuable members of society.

Teachers and students agreed that more advertising would have boosted attendance. The turnout was not as big as they wanted; no teachers attended other than those whose classes exhibited student work. Jim explained that the advertisement for the event was done at the last minute because they had focused on preparing for the event instead of advertising for it. Despite the absence of teacher visitors, quite a few teachers who knew about projects and exhibitions expressed interest in being a part of their next exhibition in June. Jim wondered whether they did not show up because they knew there would be another one as well as because of the lack of advertising. A few students responded that more exhibits and interactive stations were needed. One student suggested that they, "perhaps have a main attraction—something big and glorious!" These reflections make it evident that the seed has been planted for these students and now they desire to make exhibition bigger and better.

Asking students what could be better was a notable step, one that can put the teachers in a vulnerable position because it requires them to be open to ideas and suggestions that imply criticism. Traditional teachers seldom seek student advice or critique in how to conduct class. But the act of asking and listening can empower students to invest in their own educational experience and improve teaching.

The teachers came up with a plan for their final exhibition of the year and brought out ideas for improvement, including more ways to collaborate. When the PBL Team reflected on their first exhibition and shared their students' reflections, they considered both how the event went and how much effort it took to put it on. In that light they decided to plan for one more exhibition rather

David Ballantine,
Anderson Valley Junior Senior High School

Inspiration, Not Replication

than two more, and to hold it in June.

Jim composed an email message to all the teachers inviting them to participate in the June exhibition and sent it to everyone who had expressed interest in collaborating or showcasing their student work after the February PD sessions. In his message he set an inviting and supportive tone that would ease the fears a teacher might feel about getting involved for the first time.

In his email to the staff, Jim noted that "[e]xhibition is in some ways the final steps in a Project Based Learning curriculum, where students show off their work to the public." He described the previous exhibition, which classes presented work, and described the previous event as a "success" that they "are building on." Jim described the basics of the June exhibition event, and invited more participants to join. Jim also sought input from the staff; he wrote that he was hoping for "any way to get the students actively involved in doing an interactive demonstration or activity with the attendees." He described his hopes for collaborations between staff members and offered to share ideas with anyone interested. Towards the end, Jim's enthusiasm came through: "get students excited about exhibiting their work! Let them know about the date and get them fired up about it!"

After the April exhibition the PBL Team concluded that students should be more involved in planning and organizing the exhibition event. As a result of his class's reflections, Jim spoke with his students about having them play a more active role in the next exhibition; since the students have so much at stake during an exhibition, he thought they should also have a voice in how the event unfolds and take on a larger responsibility in the overall nature and execution of the event. Jim's students reacted positively and enthusiastically to this request. The Creation Station exhibition also changed the way teachers viewed the work they planned for the classroom.

Jim said of exhibition:

> [It] changes my focus from a project that will
> have some kind of defined endpoint—like
> turning something in or finishing building an
> object, and extends that beyond just turning it
> in. The final product becomes the exhibition,
> rather than just the product, so it's like the
> students can see their final product not as an
> isolated assignment, but part of something
> bigger from the start.

And David emphasized in his reflection that he is:

> ...definitely planning around what I thought
> was missing from this first event. I want to
> turn this into a cultural norm for the school
> and as such want them to be more frequent
> and to occur at a set amount of times per year/
> semester/quarter.

Preparing lessons and projects for an exhibition to a wide
audience gives teachers and students a greater sense of
camaraderie and purpose. For the June exhibition, Jim
planned to help the students organize themselves into
exhibition groups that will support teachers and other
students in their preparations, and also hoped that the
students would come up with a catchier name for the
event. Ultimately, Jim hoped the students would design
the entire event with support from teachers as facilitators.
Students would create and distribute advertising, organize
the exhibition spaces, and even gather necessary materials.

The Second Exhibition: E.A.R.T.H.

In preparation for the June exhibition, the PBL team revisited the areas of improvement that they wanted to address. They wanted to increase teacher participation, increase student ownership over the event, and increase the number of attendees.

In an effort to increase teacher participation, Jim sent an email to all staff inviting teachers to participate in the event. The PBL team also made personal invitations to teachers they knew were interested in the event to get them to commit to showcasing student work at the event. The result was that in total, eight teachers—but these eight teachers had more than 13 different classes present work—showcased student learning at the June exhibition of learning.

As a way to increase student ownership over the event and to ease some of the responsibilities of the PBL Team, Jim enlisted the help of one of his classes. These nine students worked with Jim to brainstorm ideas for the next exhibition and organized the logistics of the event. Jim worked behind the scenes to recruit teachers and their projects for display. When teacher interest started to solidify, Jim created a google doc spreadsheet in which teachers could put the type of project they wanted to display and number of students. The student organizational team could then use this document to plan the setup and flow of the event.

The students brainstormed names for the event and the voted. After much deliberation and negotiation the name of the event became E.A.R.T.H.:Engineering, Art, Robotics, Technology, Humanities. These students had creative control over the marketing plans and they created posters and flyers to advertise the event. Jim pointed out that having students organize the event also increased student attendance at exhibition because students wanted their friends to be a part of their experience. Even while in the throes of organizing the event and with a definitive plan, students were fervently sharing ideas for making the next event bigger and better. He noted that it was inspiring, as a teacher, to hear students periodically interject ideas and hopes they have for future exhibitions— the event was catching on and students saw value in hosting an exhibition of learning.

The day of the exhibition, the student organizers helped teachers display student work in three separate areas. Student work hung on walls, set up tabletop displays, took over grassy areas nearby, and rolled a piano outside to be the centerpiece for musical performances. There were written pieces, photographs, paintings, robots, food prepared by the culinary students, and demonstrations of dangerous equipment. The flurry of activity kept visitors engaged. The event drew approximately 120 people— three times the number of people who attended the previous exhibition. Seven teachers attended that did not have student work displayed. And students' friends and families were there to celebrate the work. A few students wished that they had "spread the word out more" and "had more of an audience." But overall, the PBL Team had 40% of their staff (eight teachers) showcase student work and increased event attendance.

After the exhibition, Jim sent out a google form survey asking participants and faculty attendees to critique the exhibition. He asked that attendees identify highlights from the event, strengths of the event, and areas that could be improved. 45 people responded; 32 of the respondents identified themselves as students.

Both students and teachers replied to the survey celebrating the diversity of student talent and learning that was displayed and the opportunity to see what others have worked on. One student wrote:

> Having live music was definitely a highlight of the event. Many people were impressed by all the talented musicians and artists. Having the tables and a few other items out on the lawn by the stage also made the area just pop more. It made it appear like a real exhibition of our work.

Audiences can have a profound effect on student performance and this student subtly pointed that out by using the word "real" to describe the event. One teacher praised the fact that this event was not just "focused on seeing your own kid's work. I love the fact that the audience was more students than parents and that the students were showing the work to each other." This same teacher later went on to say that they would like to be involved in the next exhibition. This event helped her realize the value in different audiences and making student learning public.

An exhibition can feel like a finale. As the event closes, teachers and students heave a sigh of relief as the project has been showcased, families shine with pride over their student's work, and the audience leaves having a shared experience to reflect upon. Alas, as the PBL team found out pretty quickly after both exhibitions, the next morning you awake with ideas of how and what could be done differently the next time. The next morning, Jim was approached by many students were eager to share their ideas for what to do next time and about several teachers told him they wanted to be involved in the next exhibition. A few students wanted to design a central piece or theme for the exhibition to draw community members to the event. One teacher lamented that "from what I saw it was mostly teachers and other students. It is so powerful to show off our students' works in a positive light, I really want to see the parents and community come too!" And a student reiterated this point and suggested, "...community outreach could improve. That could include more and bigger signs throughout Boonville and the rest of the Valley. I think having this as an annual event around the same time each year will also develop its reputation." Jim and the PBL Team agreed with this student's reflection and hope to start the next school year with a date in mind for a fall or winter exhibition. And so they work for the revolution.

Lessons from Anderson Valley

Build a Team

When teachers focus all their energy on grading, lesson planning, and teaching classes, their profession can be isolating. Banding together provides the structural and emotional support teachers often feel they need. Members of the original PBL Team recruited colleagues to enlarge and enrich the leadership group. David, a second-year industrial design teacher, first connected with Jim because he knew that Jim shared a classroom with Mitch called the "Media Lab." David wanted to discuss ways to make his woodshop a public access space and he was motivated by what he saw when he walked into their classrooms. He said that instead of, "sitting in rows, listening to someone talk, [students] are at completely different phases of their projects. That's what I want my wood shop to look like." Adrian, the first year Spanish teacher who was invigorated by the February PD sessions, was another recruit, attributable to the work the PBL Team put into the PD days and exhibition event.

For a small school, adding one new teacher to their PBL Team is a notable accomplishment, as there are only 20 teachers total. The June exhibition had eight teachers participate in showcasing student work and learning. In just two exhibitions the PBL Team was able to double the participation. Three teachers that attended the June exhibition, but did not participate, approached Jim in hopes of being involved in future exhibitions.

Go for It And Learn by Doing

When asked about exhibitions, HTH co-founder Rob Riordan advises:

> Just do it. Hold it in the evening, when colleagues and community can attend. Invite everyone you can think of—the mayor, school board, city council, parents, local university folks, etc. Remember that there are many skeptics who just need to see the results of PBL. Remember, too, that the students are the strongest advocates.

The Anderson Valley team had a clear expectation that they would do more than one exhibition before the end of the year. They wanted to make sure they had time to reflect, refine, and recruit for another exhibition. They worried that if they had one, it would be too easy to say, as Donna pointed out during a discussion, "'That was fun.' And then not do it again." Hosting more than one exhibition in a year also sets the expectation that there will be more in future years. The increase in teacher and student participation from the first exhibition to the second showed the team that the revolution was spreading. Jim excitedly recounted the numerous students that came up to him during the June exhibition and asked when the next one would be and "let's do this again."

After the event, collecting people's reactions and reflections to the exhibition lets everyone share their celebrations and ideas for improvement. It was upon reflection that the team cut their goal of three exhibitions down to a more manageable two exhibitions, to give teachers more time to prepare. And doing it again allows students and teachers see the growth that can occur when exhibition is tried and refined multiple times. Students were eagerly approaching Jim with ideas for the next exhibition.

Make It Public, and Advertise

The people who came to the event responded very positively. Jim, David, and Mitch specifically mentioned the impact the event had on parents of homeschooled children. Inviting community members who are interested in the student work but not directly connected to the school, or inviting those who might potentially be part of the school in the future, provides opportunities for students to share their learning with authentic audiences. The public presentation of learning is an inherently rich learning experience; students already interact with a variety of professionals and community members in the daily lives currently, and certainly will do so even more when they attend college and move on to the workplace.

One big takeaway from the PBL Team and student reflections was that the exhibition needed a lot more advertisement. They were hoping for a larger turnout, but because of competing sports events and inadequate notice, about 30 students, faculty and a sprinkling of community members attended the event. David brought up the point that there was "not enough advertising of the event and not enough lead time with the little poster we did produce." He continued, with lessons learned in marketing and community organizing:

> And the poster needs to be larger and to feature graphics of some sort, not just text. Especially if the event is new to the community, more advance notice and an eye-catching poster can draw larger crowds.

Personal invitations would likely add to the effectiveness of broadly targeted methods. Some students who had work exhibited were unable to attend because of other school events. Coordinating schedules, reserving a day, and making it special are keys to ensuring that students and families understand the importance of exhibition.

The PBL team hoped that making student work public would inspire other teachers to jump on the exhibition bandwagon. And in turn, join their PBL revolution. They have made significant progress because of their persistence in making student work public via exhibitions and because of their personal invitations to faculty. After attending the June exhibition, a teacher was grateful for the experience and imagined how they would, "showcase student work next time."

Make Students Co-designers

When the students reflected on the first exhibition they had ideas for how the next one should have a "main attraction that is big and glorious." He observed that students did not seem very excited before the first exhibition, mainly because they did not know what to expect. But after that evening they were eager to share their ideas for how to improve the exhibition experience and wanted to take a leadership role in the June exhibition. Jim took the next step and suggested that the students should design important aspects of the June event. For the June exhibition, Jim recruited one of his classes (nine students) to be the main student organizers of the event. These students were responsible for naming the event, advertising, and assisting teachers in displaying student work the day of the event. Students took ownership over the event and invited their friends and families. Jim attributed the growth in attendance to the students' efforts in advertising and organization. Student leadership was a highlight in the event, as one anonymous participant wrote in the reflection survey, "having students as docents to show and explain their work is very effective. I really loved the advertising for this event EARTH was a real winner for all the humor it generated." Facilitating student leadership in organizing the final exhibition provided extra support for the teachers who participated for the first time and gave students added incentives to do well and make the event successful, because it is now officially "their" event.

Moving PBL to the Core with Exhibition

Using exhibition as a tool for spreading PBL is challenging but worthwhile. As the Anderson Valley PBL Team found, it is not just the teachers who are the audience or advocates for spreading PBL. Students and community members become more invested in the school when they see student work publicly showcased in an effective manner. When an exhibition of learning is the culminating event in a project, teachers design their projects in anticipation of the broader audience. It can lead teachers to an important PBL design philosophy: to plan backwards from a final product. As Jim mentioned in his reflection, he looks at his lesson plans and projects differently now, knowing that families and community members will see the final products. In both the February and June exhibition, teachers displayed work from various activities or projects. Jim and the PBL team hope that with more support and experience, teachers will begin designing projects specifically for an exhibition. Donna mulled the possibilities when she wondered what would happen to student engagement if the end goal for student work was a "community audience instead of standardized tests" or a single teacher's evaluation.

In Anderson Valley, the grassroots revolution continues: the PBL Team approached the district to schedule a PBL-focused professional development time for teachers before the next school year begins. They had hoped to use this workshop to set a date for an all-school exhibition, support teachers in project creation, and conduct project tunings. However, the PBL Team's plans dramatically shifted as the school year was coming to a close. In the spring semester, the school underwent a transition in school leadership, and Jim applied for the principal's position. In June, just as the school year was ending, Jim found out that beginning next school year, he will be Anderson Valley Junior Senior High School's principal.

References and Resources

1   "School Accountability Report Card," California Department of Education, accessed February 2, 2017, http://www.avusd.k12.ca.us/Page/157.

2   "School Accountability Report Card," California Department of Education, accessed February 2, 2017, http://www.avusd.k12.ca.us/Page/157.

Henry Davenport, Warren High School

Inspiration, Not Replication

Small Steps Toward Big Changes
Transitioning to Project-Based Learning

Stephanie Lytle
High Tech High International

I t's a rainy February afternoon in Downey, California when Warren High School teachers Monica Conrad, Henry Davenport, Joy O'Dowd, and Al Zadeh wrap up their conversations with Career Pathways Project-Based Learning (PBL) Leadership Academy mentor, Kelly Jacob. They've spent the last six hours in a quiet corner office of the public high school's large administration building, coaxing hopes and ideas into cohesive project plans, and admittedly, they still need more time to think.

"It's just... a lot... to wrap my head around," Joy sighs. The self-identified Type-A anatomy and biology teacher of sixteen years is surrounded by paper pages and digital documents she has filled with carefully plotted deadlines—deadlines that she is already suspecting are subject to change. "But, I'll get it," she grins.

Since October of 2016, these four educators have committed themselves to exploring new manners of engaging the students of Warren High in learning. Selected by their administration to participate in the Career Pathways Trust PBL Leadership Academy because they were, according to math teacher Al Zadeh, "willing to try this kind of thing out," they are adapting their teaching styles to experiment with project-based learning. This is their third meeting with Kelly, and though fatigued by the everyday demands of the teaching profession, each is closing the day satisfied with the progress they have made on their project plans.

"My hope for this project," biology teacher Henry Davenport says in response to Kelly's prompting at the end of the day, "is that my students want to put their names on a piece of work that they value because it's quality work." The other three quietly nod in agreement, and then begin to pack up, making sure to share their digital files with Kelly so that she can stay in touch as they embark on their new projects. The resumed chatter is still peppered with words like "critique," "quality," and "revision" as they walk out the door and into their weekend.

The teachers have engaged in a transformation over the last few months. After gaining energy and insight through PBL Leadership Academy workshops at High Tech High in San Diego in October, they saw both buckle upon returning to school and struggling to interweave new ideas with their tight department guidelines. However, with the support of their PBL mentor and supervisors at Downey Unified, they have since regained the courage to experiment with project-based learning. This has meant taking risks by deviating from the expectations of their colleagues and their normal classroom routines. It has also meant struggling with a different way of teaching that requires both teachers and students to question why they are doing the work. The objective of project-based learning is to engage students in active learning that allows them not only to enhance their sense of agency, but to develop deeper learning competencies[1] that will extend beyond the completion of a unit, assignment, or even well-developed product. Those engaged in PBL must ask themselves tough questions. Who is the intended audience? Who will benefit from the work? How will the learning live on beyond the completion of the defined product?

Often, the conversion from a traditional, teacher-centered classroom to a PBL environment is painted as a single grand leap into teaching bliss. Students are portrayed as instantaneously engaged, self-directed learners. But, this is just not the case. The transition from one mode of teaching to another is often dotted with trials and missteps, learnings and revisions, and a lot of reflection. The teachers at Warren High bravely demonstrate this and understanding their learnings offers a valuable, and less often heard, account of the trials and hard-fought triumphs of transitioning to PBL.

How Downey Found Its Way to PBL

John Harris and Phil Davis, colleagues and friends for the past 20 years, are some of these teachers' biggest champions for change. John, Director of Curriculum, Instruction & Assessment at Downey Unified, and the former principal of Warren High, attended both PBL Leadership Academy workshops with the four teachers. Both he and Phil, a former music teacher and current Director of Support Programs, Career Technical Education (CTE), are driven not by the allure of fancy projects, but by the desire to connect students to the school through meaningful work.

"From day one, I think the focus... was connecting kids to the school program. They need to connect," John shares. Both he and Phil had unhappy K-12 experiences that they see as the source of this passion for connection. "I can only remember the name of one high school teacher.

Just one, Mrs. Matthews," John relates at the March PBL Leadership Academy conference. "The rest of the teachers didn't even think I was going to college—and acted that way.... She was the only teacher that I came in contact with that even expressed some belief that that's where I was going."

Phil, who had a similar experience with a high school music teacher, says, "For me, it has to do with kids living in the circumstances our kids live in not getting the same chance as other kids." Over the last years, all initiatives that the two have elected to support are intended to fuel Downey's students with the understanding that they are capable and worthy of producing purposeful, useful, real work not only in high school, but in college and the career they choose to pursue.

When Downey Unified was awarded the California Career Pathways Trust grant, Phil heard PBL Leadership Academy director Randy Scherer speak at a conference in Sacramento, and was encouraged to send teachers by June Bayha, the district's grant consultant and coordinator. Phil asked all Downey Unified administrators to select teachers of "core" academic subjects (math, English, etc.) who would be interested in learning more about project-based learning to attend.

Phil says of CTE teachers, "It's a non-issue, PBL. They do it. They wonder why no one else does. It's just the way you teach your class. Everything's based on the outcome of a product." His hope in bringing academic teachers to the Leadership Academy and High Tech High was for them to see how others who teach core subjects engage learners through projects.

Warren High in Downey, California

Warren High is near the "center" of Downey, California,

though really nothing within city lines is very far from the center of Downey. Approximately 111,000 residents occupy twelve square miles just thirteen miles southeast of Los Angeles. Downey was dubbed the "Mexican Beverly Hills" by the Los Angeles Times in 2015[2] because the predominantly Latino city boasts a steadily increasing median income that surpasses its big-city neighbors, but locals cry misnomer.[3] "It's literally divided by the train tracks," history teacher Monica Conrad shares. "North Downey is full of millionaire McMansions, and then there's a good portion of those on the other side who get by on food stamps." According to the LA School Report released in February of 2017, 70% of Downey students qualify for Free and Reduced Lunch.[4]

Still, Downey prides itself in offering the allure of upward mobility. Second- and third-generation immigrants have risen to the middle class over the last few decades, and this has been attributed, in part, to the city's commitment to its schools. The two high schools—just a mile apart—share an impressive 96% graduation rate, and Downey Unified is one of just two California school districts to have been designated a Partnership for 21st-century Learning (P21) exemplar district[5] because of its commitment to motivating all students to engage in "the acquisition of 21st century knowledge and skills."[6]

Warren is a large school of roughly 3,800 students and 150 staff members. Many faculty members, like Al, are also among its alumni. Academic accolades are on view, and one can go back as far as 1991 to view the "Honored Bears" not only from each department, but the overall "Leader of Tomorrow." Teachers deem it a decidedly college-applying culture, as all students are encouraged to apply to four-year universities. Each Wednesday is College Day, when students and teachers dress in college apparel. Advanced Placement (AP) courses are numerous, and school counselors urge all students to enroll.

Outside the front office, classes take place in several gray, rectangular buildings that parallel one another and offer students a chance to take in some fresh air as they walk between their 57-minute class periods. The walls are clean, but noticeably bare. The exception lies within the interior of the new science building, where the atmosphere differs slightly. A single entrance invites students into a white-walled hallway, marked by entrances to the various science rooms. Pristine bulletin boards line many of the walls. A handful are populated with remnants of recent classwork.

The Teachers

Of the four teachers, Joy O'Dowd is the member of the cohort with the longest tenure. John Harris remembers hiring the former EMT, water polo coach, and Crossfit nut sixteen years ago. Standing at only five feet tall, she is not one to be called demure. She is a careful planner and is especially concerned about making effective use of her students' time in her biology and anatomy classes. The latter is taught as preparation for those planning to study medicine. "Her anatomy [class] is way different than the anatomy I took in high school," colleague Monica Conrad acknowledges. Joy's classroom features student work from recent projects, which she occasionally displays in the hallways of the science building. Joy, who requires her students to document their work on websites, came to the October workshop looking for ways to use this platform to reach a larger audience for her students. "So often they do it for the grade," she says. "I want them to do good work."

Henry Davenport, a 2005 graduate of neighboring Downey High, also teaches biology. A tall, soft spoken man with long, wavy hair, he connects easily with his students and is eager to make school different. Like his parents before him, he enrolled in community college before transferring to a four-year university. As a high school student, he was not enrolled in the rigorous AP courses that many of his friends took. Because he saw many of them fail to get their degrees, he constantly considers whether his students are engaging in true, deeper learning or simply working for the grade.

Monica Conrad, who also graduated from Downey High, was one of those students enrolled in the AP courses, but attributes her deep connection with history to her own background. The daughter of Cambodian refugees, the US and World History teacher opens her classes each year with the story of her family's hardships. You will not find these stories in history books, she tells them, and this is why she teaches history. She hopes her students will understand that history is not always recorded correctly.

Al Zadeh is also 2007 graduate of Warren High. Joy was his teacher and coach. A cheerful, welcoming man with a kind smile, he is beginning his first year at his alma mater after teaching math at Alliance College-Ready Public schools.

All four teachers are not only involved with the core classes, but have dedicated their time to supporting students in additional roles, such as Project Lead the Way, LINK Crew, and robotics.

Initial Excitement

When the four attended PBL Leadership Academy in October with John Harris and June Bayha, they were energized, to say the least. Workshops on evaluation and critique and and the "Environmentalists Adrift" project became ideals that they believed their school could strive for, and as June Bayha recalls, the four were eager to share their learnings with the staff at Warren High.

"They had some pretty ambitious goals. They wanted things school-wide to change," she recalls. With plans to lead the staff in a session on providing meaningful feedback, they were, according to June, "gung ho to try something."

But, it wasn't quite as easy as they had hoped. Their initial excitement was squashed when they weren't able to book a time slot with the administration to lead the all-staff training. Dismayed, they looked for ways to implement projects within their classrooms, but felt inhibited by the expectations that they follow their respective departments' pacing guides (jointly determined curricula with timelines). They struggled to determine a way to teach the same content at the same time as their colleagues and to design and implement a project that would allow them to do so.

"What we're told in our department meetings," Henry explained, "is, 'We're on this subject now. We're doing that for four weeks, and then we're going to move on to this.'" At this point, the four wanted to experiment with project-based learning, but were unsure of how to make the transition while simultaneously aligning with the timing and practices of their department colleagues.

Getting Started

A month after the conference, Henry boldly dove into his first project and let loose his grasp on the department pacing guide. He presented his biology students with the question "How do we reduce the carbon footprint at Warren High School?" and a project was born. Students brainstormed as many ways as they could think of to address the concern before selecting one that they would research in a team of four and pitch to an audience of administrators.

Over the next month, students not only researched solutions, but were calling local companies, asking for information about solar panels, solar trash cans, trash compactors, and the like. One group secured a speaker from the LA County organization, Tree People, to talk with them about their composting project. This was a tremendous departure from Henry's usual practice of staying aligned with the biology department's pacing guide. When the time came for students to pitch their solutions to a group of administrators in December, though, Henry was not feeling victorious.

"I thought I failed," he said, noting all the things he hadn't considered. Groups of four turned out to be too large for this particular project, leaving some with more idle time than others. On the flip side, some of the students' ideas were so big that they didn't have time to build a model or make an extensive plan that would allow them to test their ideas. "So, when they got to that point, they were like, 'How are we supposed to do that?'"

They were running up against finals, and Henry gave students a rubric for the presentations, but did not have enough class time for preparation and critique. "I thought we didn't have time because I had to have a project done for finals, or, you know—grades," he says. On the big day, their presentations fell short of the expectations Henry had set forth. He attributes this to not carving out enough time for critique. Embarrassed and disheartened, he was having a hard time looking past some of the shortcomings of his first project and seeing the small, but substantial shift in his classroom.

The Need for Support

Through her communications with the WHS team, PBL Leadership Academy mentor Kelly Jacob noted that the team's spirits had fallen since the October workshop and reached out to schedule a work day to meet with the four teachers, plus June, John, and Phil. It had been nearly six weeks since even the teachers had been able to sit in the same room together, and they were losing steam. "They were bought in, they went back, and they were like—BAM—into a wall," June observed. The four felt stuck. They had a pacing guide that their colleagues expected them to follow, but now they had hopes to engage their students differently, and they felt they were falling short of their own high expectations.

"It's really hard to do in our big school," Joy lamented as the December morning turned into what Kelly felt was akin to a group therapy session. The teachers had tried, and perceived themselves to have failed, and this was the first time they had been in shared space to safely acknowledge their struggles. Monica, Joy, and Al had not yet implemented a project, and Henry felt that his attempt had been a failure. When he lamented the pitfalls of his carbon footprint project, Kelly was taken aback by how hard he was on himself. "It was really interesting because I didn't see this as failure at all. He shot for the moon and landed somewhere in the galaxy," she shared, noting that the work he had done revealed a lot of new learning.

> Students got a choice. You got to watch students absolutely engaged in a project. Did they present to a professional audience? Yes, they did. Maybe not the city council of Downey, but the school administration. There was the sense that we're doing something for a bigger audience and a bigger cause, and not just because Mr. Davenport told us we had to do it for a project.

Though reassured by her words, the four really needed affirmation from their superiors at the district office, Phil and John.

"Failing once is learning," Phil offered, reminding Henry that, as a science teacher, he should be okay with that. "So, what's happened so far is all good stuff," he told them. "So you weren't successful. Well, we'll figure it out. Now's your time to figure stuff out."

Phil's assurance went a long way. "You could see [Henry] kind of re-evaluate," Kelly said. "If he hadn't had that failure, I don't think he would have been pushing himself right now to the extent that he is because he saw pieces of it worked."

These pieces can be difficult to cling to, and teachers can be tempted to let them fall through their fingers and reach back for the comfort of their regular classroom routine— even when they know that it isn't working either. The discomfort of transitioning from one mode of teaching to another was obscuring Henry's ability to build on the small successes he had experienced.

The group also sensed a collective despair at the pressure from their colleagues to stay on the same page. Henry explained,

> So, like for biology right now, we're supposed to be on homeostasis and human body systems. But I'm on DNA and genetics. So, everyone's like "Are you almost done with the immune system?" and I don't want to tell them [that I am not] because the culture has been... "Why are you doing something different?" But, I'm doing it because of this [PBL Leadership Academy].

Kelly feared that the team was about to backpedal again.

> There was this moment in the meeting when I looked at Phil, and I said, "Phil, I think what

they need is you to say, "You have approval to go off the pacing guide. You have approval to try and fail." And he gave it to them. Literally... you kind of saw their faces change. You saw the mood change, and immediately, the computers start opening, and it was Joy who was like, "Okay. Let me show you this." It was palpable, the difference.

Rebounding

When the four teachers met with Kelly two months later, their spirits were much higher. Knowing they had the support of their district supervisors had given them the courage to continue experimenting with PBL. Henry had decided to focus on the pieces of his carbon footprint project that worked and encouraged the marine biology club he advises to pick up the compost project that was selected as the most viable way to reduce the school's carbon footprint. The students were using a toolkit provided by Tree People, the organization that supported the students' work, to interview people on campus. They had also received a $200 grant from Jane Goodall's Roots and Shoots youth service learning program to buy compost tumblers. As of February, they were collecting scraps for the compost tumblers from the culinary arts department and the cafeteria.

When Kelly commented on Henry's positivity, he admitted that he had come to see the benefits of his own learning. Though difficult, he shares,

> I think it was just a justification that I should do that kind of stuff rather than I can't do it. So, instead of trying to give a test that we're all giving on the same day because we're all teaching biology, it was like, 'no, I can do this project; it's fine.' But, that was from you guys

[Kelly and High Tech High], and the workshop, and John and Phil.

Timing is Everything

That morning, Henry was ready to move forward and discuss a new project idea. In order to learn more about how hereditary diseases and conditions affect one's lifestyle, students would be creating a story of a fictional character who discovers he or she has one of the conditions Henry had selected. Henry had already created a model of the written product and contacted Woodsnap, a local company that prints photos onto wood, to print the students' portraits of their characters to be exhibited at a local art gallery. Kelly was impressed at how he had bounced back from his perceived failure with the carbon footprint project, and the two began to look for ways to avoid some of the mistakes he made in his first project.

This time students would be working individually in an effort to keep everyone engaged for the duration of the project. Each student would be in charge of creating a character, researching the condition he or she would receive, writing the story of his or her experience with the condition, and then creating a portrait of this character. Henry remained uncertain of the timing. During his last project, he did not feel he built in enough time for critique sessions and attributed the students' lackluster presentations to this. This time, he was hoping to give students sufficient time, but this was still new to him, and he needed to know from Kelly how much time was enough.

> Henry: When I started, I was like, oh, I'll do this for like two months or something. But, because I want quality, I'm thinking maybe the rest of the year... Or at least April.
>
> Kelly: When's your spring break?

Henry: April 14th.

Kelly: I think that's as far back as I'd possibly push it... Do you guys have finals?

Henry: We have testing. Two weeks of testing in April, and then spring break is the third week.

Kelly: So that gives you a pretty clear deadline, then. I think you need to be done by March 31st. That's eight weeks from today. I think eight weeks is a really reasonable time. If you devote too much time to it—

Henry: It gets boring.

Kelly: Right. You need traction.

Pacing a Project

Many PBL teachers are rightly concerned about pacing a project. How do you keep students engaged in the immediacy of a project while allowing time to try, fail, revise, and critique? Jeff Robin, art teacher at High Tech High, advises that teachers do the project first themselves to fully understand the pace and process.[7] Then, the teacher accounts for his or her own level of expertise in the subject matter. For example, it may take an adult professional just one week to complete a project, but a student, who is likely a novice, will need far more time—the student is addressing questions that the adult answered long ago, and learning skills and content that the adult has mastered. When teachers do the project first, they can predict these teachable moments.

There is no perfect mathematical equation to determine the best length of time for a project, but Kelly brings up important points. One, it's good to complete a project before a large break in a schedule to prevent students from losing traction. Second, if a project deadline is set too far out, then the sense of immediacy is lost and time can be squandered. Still Henry was set on righting his former mistake and giving them enough time to settle into the project, criticize each other's work constructively, and complete something they feel pride in. "A quality final project will make them feel connected to the individual [character], will take them on a journey through what the character's been through in their life so far," he says. He's after quality final products, but he's also after empathy.

Projects That Can Be Of Use

Kelly chose to push Henry on the utility of his planned project. She commended his efforts to have his students create a fictional character through whom the class and those who attend their exhibition connect to the challenges associated with a genetic condition. However, she'd like to see them create something that can also be used by audience members. She suggested that students create a website that will provide resources for those who discover that they or a loved one have one of the specified conditions.

> Kelly: I was thinking of how to get them from just something that the students create, that won't really be looked at again after the project is completed, to something that could actually be useful and continue to be of value.

> Henry: Informational.

> Kelly: I really wanted to focus in on extending the learning beyond the classroom. So

potentially it might be really beneficial to somebody like, for example, my mother-in-law who got diagnosed with Parkinson's, and we didn't know what to do. I mean, who do you talk to? Where do you go? So maybe one of those pages could be that. They have to have their bio, which would be their character bio. They have to have a page of resources where can people go to find information on XYZ, and then something like an empathy interview page. Like what was it like to experience being told that....

Henry: So how would it affect you or your family member? And then tips to educate the public and raise awareness about the disease or disorder?

Kelly: Perfect.

The two continued to discuss how this webpage could be used as a resource for those afflicted with the conditions that the students' characters will have. But, building a website and conducting interviews will require additional planning and scheduling that Henry hadn't accounted for. He'll need to gather models for the prospective website and connect his students with people in the community who have these conditions. Admittedly, he'll have some work to do that will require thinking and action beyond the time he has allotted with his coach today.

Kelly also helped Joy with the same challenge. Joy hoped to have her biology and anatomy class track their own eating habits on a personal website before then writing an evaluation of their own eating habits. Additionally, students would explore various avenues of wellness that they will document on the same site. Additionally, students would explore various avenues of wellness that they will document on this same site. After considering options and recognizing the time available, Joy accepted Kelly's suggestion that her students sponsor a "mini wellness fair" where groups of students are in charge of presenting one element of wellness to undergraduates who cycle through each station. The guests at the fair will be an additional source of critiques of her students' work, along with parents and peers.

In the Thick of It—and Feeling Positive

When we walk into Henry's biology classroom in March, he is feeling much more optimistic than he was last December. What's changed? Not only has he gathered some tips and tricks by reflecting on the pitfalls of his previous carbon footprint project, but his students are adjusting to project-based learning, and his department colleagues are intrigued by what he is doing.

Hierarchy of Audience

Ron Berger, of EL Education and the Harvard Graduate School of Education, is a proponent of celebrating student learning with authentic audiences. He contends that these events require students to reflect on and articulate not only what they learned, but how they learned.

Berger contends that when students are asked to present to an audience outside of their classroom, they are motivated to produce high quality work. The presence of a public audience affirms that students' work can affect those beyond the walls of their school, and increasingly authentic and significant audiences motivate ever higher quality and more meaningful work. At the top of Berger's hierarchy of audiences for student work and learning lies "to be of service in the world."[8]

Purposeful changes to organizational strategies have contributed to this newfound optimism. Whereas during his fall carbon footprint project, he had looser, weekly deadlines, he now utilizes a daily to-do list. Not only does this reduce confusion, but the tighter deadlines actually allow for more flexibility. "When they wouldn't have it done, I would just move forward because I thought I was on a time limit," he explains. Now, he is able to see when students are off target more quickly and make necessary changes to the schedule. Because his students have grown accustomed to working on their own as Henry circulates and offers support, he is able to address students' challenges and concerns more immediately.

He is also learning to be patient as students create their final projects. Though he has a checklist of information that should be included on the web pages, he is trying to step back and allow students to personalize their deliverables. He knows that it's important to share his high expectations for the final product, but even more important to consider the learning that is happening while they are working on it. "It's not all about the webpage or the presentation; it's about everything that goes on in between," he says. This time, he plans to incorporate extensive student reflection, which helps "calm [him] down" when he sees students veering from his expectations.

Indeed, students are learning. "I didn't even know what 'pedigree' was before this," ninth-grader Kayla shares. "I thought he was talking about the dog food," she grins. As they research conditions ranging from Huntington's disease to Parkinson's to bipolar disorder, they are not only conducting research and utilizing software from Progeny Genetics to discover how the disease can be passed on. They are also learning about the challenges of those they know personally. One student, whose character discovers he has testicular cancer, now has a better understanding of the disease that may have personally affected her middle school dean. She shares, "He used to play basketball and sports and all that, and when he found out, it limited him to a lot of things that he had to give up. So, now I know a little more about what he was going through."

Most notably, the sense of ownership of their projects has escalated. Henry relates that students are extremely attached to their characters because "It's them, almost. It's like what they want to be. A lot of them, when I ask, are you attached to that character? They're like, 'Yeah, I made that character.' They feel invested."

Most students acknowledge that it's a different kind of learning than they have experienced. Deanna, a tenth-grader, admitted that when Henry first told her about the project, "I was like, I don't know what I'm going to do. Like, I don't think I can make a person up." But once they fight past this initial hesitation, most feel like Deanna, who relates, "I thought it was going to be harder to make somebody. I just started putting stuff together, just thinking." Students admit that it also requires a lot of research, which, once you get the hang of it, they say, is easy. "I think that it does take time, but once you get it and you understand it, it's pretty much easy," ninth-grader Xenia shares. "Normally, we do book work," another says. "Boring stuff. This is better. I like this class. I just feel this is more interesting than some of the other stuff that other classes do."

Henry has also noticed that he doesn't have to worry about students copying one another's work. Because each is creating something new and different, there is no way for them to simply pass another's work off as their own. "There's a few people that are looking at each other's and asking each other, 'What are you doing? Do you know how to do this?' But that's good," he insists, because they are finding ways to give each other feedback.

Henry's colleagues are still asking questions, but their tone has changed to one of curiosity about his work. During his most recent meeting, he shares, "I wasn't even going to talk about it at the meeting, and then one of the teachers was like, 'What about that project you're doing?' And then, everybody else was like, 'What are you doing?'" Though they were concerned about how he was able to cover the content required by the pacing guide, he replied that he was covering everything, at an admittedly slower pace. He was able to share his thoughts on the need for the pacing guide, which John Harris insists is a curricular map that needs to be flexible. "It was kind of weird," he exclaims, "because [for the first time] they were like, 'Oh, we could do stuff like this.' So, that was kind of cool, too. And I didn't expect that."

Henry still has many wonderings. How can he encourage students to strike the right balance between providing valuable content and engaging visuals? What is the best way to assess students' learnings? But, his confidence is growing and spreading to that of his colleagues and students. As they prepare for their upcoming exhibition, he is excited for the excitement the students' work is sure to generate. He has also found a benefactor in Woodsnap, a local printing company that offered to print students' portraits of their characters on a piece of wood for free. Though his plans to display these at a local art gallery didn't materialize, he now plans to display them on the blank white walls that line the hallway outside his classroom. In this way, students will get to show off their work to their peers and they hope, passersby will become curious.

Starting Small and Building Out

History teacher Monica Conrad decided to start small. She chose to begin her first project with her SkillsUSA class, which, unlike her history classes, does not have a pacing guide. SkillsUSA classes focus on preparing students for the workforce and align with career technical education (CTE). As such, she wanted to prepare her students not only to be interviewed, but to conduct interviews.

"It really worked out," she said, "because a lot of them don't know what they really want to do, and they don't quite know know their own history and reality at the same time." So, just as she would do to her history students at a later date, she charged them with interviewing someone who had immigrated to the United States.

Monica made sure to prep them extensively for the interviews, but in a manner that made students think deeply about how they would want to be treated as interviewees. She wanted to teach them about active listening, so she asked them to share how they would like someone to treat them if they were asking them a question. Together, students came up with a checklist. "And then," Monica says, "I kind of turned it on them by saying, 'Well, this is what you should do while you're doing this project,'" reminding them that a huge component of the project is to "gain perspective and understand the other side of the wall." This led to a conversation about doing some preliminary research on the place their interviewee emigrated from. Once this was completed, Monica provided students with a list of questions that were meant to be a guide. They worked with partners to customize their list of questions so that they felt personalized to the interviewee and then they practiced how to broach sensitive topics.

Monica feels a key part of the preparation was relating how she talked to her own father about his immigration story.

> I gave them his background of being in a
> [Cambodian] genocide and living through that.
> He talked about the hardships of the journey

Monica Conrad, Warren High School

he had to take just to come to this country. And then, he had a lot of hardships here. And they kinda just went, 'I don't even know my parent's story.' Or, 'I don't even know my grandparents' story.' And I said, 'That's perfect because that's the whole point of this! I want you to understand the story behind the person.'

She went on to discuss how they should photograph their interviewee, as well. The photograph, she explained, should be reflective of their experience. "And I said, for my dad, it's not his face that tells his story; it's his hands. Like, the calluses, the cuts."

Because Downey has such a large population of immigrants, it was not very difficult for students to find interviewees. Of the 3800 students currently at Warren High, Monica estimates that at least a hundred are immigrants. Immigration is a big part of Downey's history, and therefore a big part of their own. Some students are interviewing friends, while others are interviewing teachers or friends of family members. Still others are interviewing their mothers, fathers, grandmothers, and grandfathers, unearthing brand new information that they wouldn't have without this project.

Tenth-grader Danny shared about his grandfather, "I thought he wouldn't want to talk about it, but I told him it was for a project. I was surprised that he went through all that stuff and still came here... I'm really impressed by that."

Another student shared that while his father had always been fairly open about his experience being born in Mexico to a Czech father and Mexican mother, he was still able to learn new things.

He told me it was rough growing up in

Mexico, and I asked him to what extent it was rough. He said it was very segregational to an extent because they were looking at him very differently [as a man with blond hair and blue eyes]. So I found out that my dad decided to learn Tae Kwon Do, and he ended up becoming one of the national champions, and I didn't know that... He's my dad. He takes me to school. He goes to work.... It was pretty big.

Still others learned more about peers. Monica says, "One of my kids just turned to the person who sits next to him in class and said, 'Can I interview you? I know that you're doing the same project, but what about your story?'" Monica was thrilled because she felt like they were moving toward a point where they realized they could teach one another through their own shared histories.

After beginning the project with her SkillsUSA class, she felt comfortable moving the project into her US and World History classes. Although she kept many of them same elements, the lens was bit different. A running theme in her history classes has been to examine how particular groups of peoples were subject to discrimination during particular moments in history. As they moved into their study of WWII, they had been discussing how Japanese internment camps were created because this group was perceived as a threat. As students spoke to their interviewees, they were instructed to look for how this person was treated based upon where and when they emigrated.

Her students clearly felt the responsibility to accurately capture interviewee's stories. Maricela said, "I felt like a little journalist because I was taking notes, and I have the recording. So, this was really interesting." When asked if she would recommend the project to others, she said, "It could open their eyes up to new possibilities, hardships that other people have gone through, and it might even motivate them to continue doing this as a career."

Monica is still working on how she will collect all of these stories and showcase them, but is happy that students are already sharing their interviewees' stories with one another.

> I've seen them talk to people, to their classmates, too about, "What was your person's story?" And they're like, "Oh, that's so different from my person's story." They're teaching each other. That connection and that knowledge, they are kind of sharing with each other.

She plans to begin by capitalizing on this and host a classwide gallery walk of the students' portraits, interviews, and reflections. But after that, she's not sure. She contemplates using a self-publishing site to pull together the interviews either by time period or geographic location, or contacting a local oral history project to house the interviews--something she had discussed with HTH mentor, Kelly, during their last meeting.

Ideally, the audience would have been determined before the project began, but Monica had planned to start small. Next time, she says, she feels as though she might be able to go bigger. But because she started in a smaller space with less pressure, she says that her first foray into project-based learning wasn't as intimidating or as time-consuming as she had feared. Initially, she says:

> I was a little hesitant because there was just that fear of dealing with [department] pressures, the common assessments. Like, how do I still focus on that and then give this project a chance? I think starting it out in the smaller SkillsUSA class helped out.

Empathy and Social Learning

Both Monica Conrad and Henry Davenport were hoping for their students to not only take ownership over their learning, but to experience empathy for those within their school and broader community. Thom Markham, founder and CEO of PBL Global, insists that empathy "lies at the heart of 21st century skillfulness" in our increasingly connected world. Monica's project aimed to connect her students to a range of immigration experiences so that, together, they could construct an understanding of an important part of Downey's history and the plight faced by those who immigrated there. Working first with a community member to collect knowledge and understanding, and then working to share this with their peers allowed students to build empathy and the sense of responsibility to share their newfound understanding with their peers.

This kind of social learning, first cited by Albert Bandura, not only allows students to understand what happened in their history, but how others felt about it. Furthermore, students were offered the opportunity to share and build an understanding of the immigration experience that would allow them to consider the shortcomings of the immigration system itself, thus propelling them to consider alternatives. In this way, students are "forg[ing] deep connections [which] lead to creative problem solving and positive pursuits" that Markham deems necessary for 21st century learners.

Struggling with Scheduling

When we meet with Joy O'Dowd as she prepares for her Human Body Systems course, she is struggling with scheduling. She has decided to forego the walkthrough she had previously planned with Kelly when a school lockdown caused her to lose a day of her tightly packed schedule.

Her students agree that it helps. Twelfth-grader Brianna explains:

> I think it [critique] is good because sometimes you don't really know things that you're missing or things that you're doing really well unless someone else tells you. I feel like I get good feedback from my peers because everyone's really honest.

Joy has established a culture of high expectations and trust that enables this feedback to be fruitful, and it's working. After her most recent experience, she took the time to cross-reference the feedback they received from their peers and the changes made on their websites, and found that students are, in fact, making the changes suggested.

In an effort to encourage students to share their work with people outside the classroom, she asked family members and guardians to complete the same critique form at home. She was dismayed by a less than two-thirds return rate, and isn't sure whether to attribute this to the students or their guardians' lack of follow-through. Still, those who did get critiques, like Brianna, clearly benefited. "It's usually just small talk about school," she says, "but actually showing [my aunt] what I do is kind of cool. But you kind of stress out a little because what if they don't like it?" This healthy level of stress is just what

Al Zadeh, Warren High School

Inspiration, Not Replication

the showcasing of work is meant to do. It forces students to consider how an audience will receive their work. It also allows for them to talk about their work and to share their new understandings with someone who may benefit from hearing them. Brianna's conversation with her aunt led to a discussion of wellness. Says Brianna:

> I think there's a lot of stereotypes that wellness is just one thing—like physical wellness. But, when [her aunt] looked at [my website], she was like, 'Yeah... just because you're good physically doesn't mean that mentally you're okay emotionally.' So, there's a lot of factors that have to do with overall wellness. There's a stereotype that there's only one kind of wellness, and that's all that matters.

Students have had the opportunity for at least three other people to view their website, and when we left Joy she was still contemplating how to make the websites more visible to others without compromising students' privacy. She has seen a difference in the way students view their work. She says:

> I think there is pride in them showing their work. Because in the past, they've done it for me, and they've done it for a grade. So, this is the first year that I've had them showcase, and I've had them share with three or four people.

Her students are enjoying it and want more. Says Brianna, "I would like to look at others' sites not to critique them, but to go, 'Oh, that's really cool that you did that.'" Joy has some thinking to do about whether she will stay the course of the curriculum or relinquish a couple days for students to do just that.

Adapting an Existing Lesson

Like Monica, Al is taking smaller, purposeful steps as he and his students work on their first project together. He is building on an existing activity from the online resource mathalicious.com that calls for his ninth-grade integrated math students to use systems of equations to calculate, compare, and graph the amount of money a high school graduate is likely to make over the course of his or her lifetime to the amount of money one who has an Associate's, Bachelor's, and Master's degree is likely to earn. Once all students complete this, each will select two different career paths that he or she is considering. They will determine the average salary earned in the profession of their choice and select a school or program they would like to attend to earn the required degree. Then, using the same equations, they will calculate, compare, and graph the amount of money they are likely to earn in each of these paths. They will display their findings on tri-fold boards for an in-school exhibition of learning for students in the school's AVID program, which is designed to close the achievement gap and give all students the tools to succeed in college.

When we sit down with him in March, Al is happy with how things are going. He is learning more about students as they share their desired careers, and he feels that when they share their online research they are learning from one another about different schools and pathways after high school. "That's information that they didn't have before," says Al, "and that's information they are getting with this project. It's getting the ball rolling. At least they're in that mindset that college is within reach." When students are in this mode of researching and sharing with one another, the overall tone of the class has felt different. Diana, who is researching schools that will allow her to pursue her dream to become a director, shares that a typical day in math class is usually, "We have units, and each day we do the lesson and worksheet. And then we have homework." This Friday, however, students are working with their table groups of four to understand the system of equations they will need to use to calculate the monetary value associated with their desired careers. Though she acknowledges that she does learn quite a bit through Al's lessons, she prefers the atmosphere that fills the classroom during project time. "I like projects because you work with your table group, and you can get creative."

Al has also appreciated the "vibe" of the classroom as students are buzzing and sharing information with one another. Because dedicating a large amount of class time to group work and project time is a departure from the regular routine of his classroom, he is being careful to strike a balance between "covering the material" and "project time." Initially, he did so because his department colleagues insisted he would not be able to carve out time from their planned curriculum to complete the project. He compromised, and, for the next couple weeks, plans to dedicate half of his class time to the lessons agreed upon by his department and the other half to the project.

The project, however, is connected to the current curriculum. "We just finished this lesson, this content," he says. "It was finding slope, y-intercept, graphing. So, it's graphing, making tables.... It's called systems of equations. That's the whole lesson." His colleagues' resistance gave him pause, but with the support of Kelly and his three colleagues he decided to go for it, hoping that what they learned would stay with students over the long haul.

> I think that students will definitely remember it when they're juniors, seniors. [I hope they say], 'I remember doing this project in Mr. Zadeh's class, and I realized I can make a million

dollars more if I go to college, and that's when I realized I wanted to be a nurse or a doctor.' So, I think that's a good key takeaway that I want to instill in the kids, so, why not do the project?

His students are definitely getting that message. Raul, who plans to be a firefighter, says, "When we first started it, he was telling us that this would be important to us because it would help us on which college and what degree we'll do." Al is also making room for discussion about the value they attach to those numbers that they calculate. "It's not all about money," Al says, "but what makes you happy. So, that's another piece in the project that they see and research." He draws on his own career experience, beginning as a civil engineer, and how he ultimately decided to be a teacher.

Though the initial plan was for students to display their work at the school's career fair, which would have reached a larger audience, he is excited to start small with a group of AVID students and their other teachers. Even his department colleagues are taking note of how just a few small adjustments to an important component of the math curriculum have allowed for personalization and brought in an authentic audience. A colleague even plans to try the project after Al completes it. "So, by that point, I'll be able to give him pointers. Like, 'This worked; this didn't,'" he says. "So, it's planting a seed with other teachers."

Al and his students have kept their grounding by simply pivoting in small ways. And this bodes well for them. He has taken a much different approach than Henry, who felt more suited to diving into an entirely different way of being in the classroom. As teachers decide to take on these new practices, it's important to consider that there is no single way to do it. Some might decide to wade into it, while others will cannon ball. All four teachers have grown in different ways over the course of the last six months, and their growth has had quite the effect on their students and the larger school community.

Lessons Learned: Small Steps to Big Changes

Over the last few months, Henry, Joy, Monica, and Al have made small, but significant changes to their teaching practices. As they shifted their focus from keeping up the same pace as their department colleagues to designing opportunities for students to make deep, personal connections to the content, they struggled with discomfort. Their struggle unearthed several lessons for others hoping to transition to PBL.

We All Make Mistakes

Teachers are famously tough critics of themselves. They hold themselves to high standards because they so value the people they aim to serve. What they sometimes forget is that they, too, are learners. And just as they encourage students to see their failures as learning opportunities if they tried wholeheartedly, they must remember to do the same. Though Henry perceived his first project as a failure, Kelly was quick to highlight the strengths of his design and areas for improvement for next time. More important, she insistently reminded him that he took an important risk in deciding to alter his teaching with the larger goal of engaging his students in the kind of deeper learning he felt was lacking within his curriculum.

Teachers who view fabulous student work produced under the leadership of an experienced project designer are inclined to hope that they can generate the same results by immediately modifying their instructional practices. The experience of the Warren teachers demonstrates that it's important to collect small wins and re-evaluate losses while modestly shifting teaching methods. In April, Henry remarked that it was easy to get scared and shut down when his first experience was less than ideal. He attributed his willingness to persist to the positive and constructive feedback he received from his mentor, Kelly, and from district supervisors Phil and John. "I'm somebody who is coachable," he says, "and I want criticism, whether it's good or bad, so I can do it better." The coaching and support provided enabled him to reframe missteps as learnings and encouraged him to design his second project, one he felt was a marked improvement from his first.

Support is Needed

All teachers agreed that the time spent with Kelly and the other staff members at the PBL Leadership Academy, and the time for collaboration were invaluable to their growth this year. Upon returning to Warren after the October conference, their optimism and bravery plummeted in the face of questioning colleagues and perceived failures. Six weeks had passed since all had been able to sit in the same room together, and the teachers were craving coaching from Kelly, reassurance from their supervisors, and renewed camaraderie with one another. "Having the support to fire off questions and get suggestions [from Kelly] was invaluable," Joy insists.

As a teacher in the first few years of his career, Henry not only appreciated the coaching, but the support from his superiors. "We are all learners," he says, "and we are all trying to learn how to teach. So, when HTH and John and Phil were very supportive, it made me feel like I could do this."

As for Phil and John, they do recognize their influence, but are insistent that these teachers have greater power than they have to change school culture. Top-down strategies will die when their leaders move on to different positions, but small movements from those in the trenches will breed long-lasting success and generate interest from others. "The only people that are going to be interested in contributing to and fixing [flaws within a school program] are the ones who own it and have their fingerprints on it," John says. Thus, in encouraging these four teachers to take risks, the two administrators hope that others may follow suit and find new and better ways to engage their students in deeper learning.

Examine What You're Doing and Why

Throughout the time that Kelly worked with these teachers, they kept naming one thing that they felt stood in their way of fully engaging in a project: their department's pacing guides. When they had their first meeting with Kelly, after having fallen short of their lofty post-conference goals, they all discussed their fear of deviating from their colleagues' routine of teaching and testing the same topic at the same time. Even though John, as director of secondary curriculum, reassured them that they were permitted to spend additional time on a project that might mean curtailing their original plans, they were hesitant. John found this interesting and observed that it seemed to be coming from a lingering district norm that has since changed, even noting that the term, "pacing guide," hadn't been used in professional development for the last two years. Instead, departments are encouraged to share a "curriculum map," that he insists is meant to be used as a tool and not a prescription.

The lingering practice of sticking to the no-longer existent pacing guide is something that he suspects has become part of the "hidden curriculum," or unspoken expectations that have become enveloped in the school's culture. Warren High has extraordinarily low teacher turnover, which means many of its teachers were coached to follow the pacing guide in order to deliver a consistent curriculum at a time when common and consistent assessments were encouraged by district staff. The curriculum map, though, allows for teachers to implement their own strategies and abide by their own schedule to teach the content. Still, this is not how many Warren teachers understand it. This disconnect meant that our four teachers felt they were taking a huge risk in deviating from the plans of their department colleagues.

John suspects that district staff didn't spend enough time addressing why curriculum maps were being used, which led teachers to be concerned about following them rather than using them as a tool. By the same token, the implementation of a project should not be viewed as the sole strategy for engaging learners in deeper learning. Doing so simply replaces curriculum maps with projects as a new dogma. Teachers must ask themselves why the strategy implemented offers their students an optimal connection to developing new skills and understanding new content.

Students Must Own Their Learning

Because of the risk they took to alter their curriculums, our teachers saw their students engage in a kind of deeper learning they hadn't previously seen. Through the coaching they received from Kelly, each teacher designed a project that allowed for students to personalize their experience in such a manner that they then could share their learnings with one another, effectively becoming both learners and teachers.

In Henry's class, students first created fictional characters that often were loose representations of themselves or the world they knew. Because Henry had coached them on creating a character they came to know intimately, when it came time for the character's condition to be revealed, the students were driven to discover how this new impediment might thwart the hopes they had built for these characters. Because each student's character received a different genetic condition, they were able to teach one another how these conditions varied. Thus, students were able to own the character they created. This emotional attachment made them care about the biology they learned.

Monica's history students were offered the opportunity to become young historians on a topic of immediate interest to the local community. Downey's influx of immigrants in the last few decades gave them lots of stories to capture and share, and each student was able to become an expert on one community member's story. Then they were in charge of sharing this with the class, allowing the class to collectively exam the similarities and differences among their immigrant neighbors.

Likewise, Al's integrated math students were able to personalize the math they learned by using it in connection with college and career pathways of their choice. Their exhibition of learning for the AVID group afforded them the opportunity to impart their learning to others beyond the classroom.

Each of these projects required a pivot from normal classroom routine, but proved manageable by both teachers and students. Projects enabled students to incorporate a personal interest and then share their learnings with their peers, two ways of accomplishing exactly what these teachers were after—allowing students to own their learning.

Next Steps

Moving forward, each teacher would like to find ways for students' work to connect more closely to the school and local community. Though they found audiences for students' work, they are now looking forward to the opportunity to plan ahead for fall projects so that more students are able to work toward a defined purpose. Though the audience and final product should be clear, they also hope to continue crafting thoughtful essential questions to launch each product. Says Henry, "I'm definitely going to start each unit with a big question that's not able to be answered simply. Or it may seem simple, but when you really start talking about it, it's not."

Moving forward, each teacher recognizes that decisions about how to transition to project-based learning must be in service of the young learners they work with. Each year, new students join the community, changes happen within the city, and in the world at large. Teaching, too, must change. While listening to keynote speaker Emily Pilloton of Project H at the PBL Academy Leadership Institute at HTH in March, John scribbled the quote "When you are through changing, you are through." The teachers of Warren High show us that engaging students in deeper learning requires braving the struggles and risks associated with adapting their teaching, step-by-step, to the times and to the children we serve.

References and Resources

1   "Deeper Learning," William and Flora Hewlett Foundation, http://www.hewlett.org/strategy/deeper-learning/.

2   C. Carcamo, "Latinos' Rising Fortunes Are Epitomized in Downey," *Los Angeles Times*, August 5, 2015, http://www.latimes.com/local/la-me-downey-latinos-20150805-story.html.

3   T. Vasquez, "No, Downey Is Not 'Mexican Beverly Hills,'" *The Downey Patriot*, August 6, 2015, http://www.thedowneypatriot.com/articles/no-downey-is-not-mexican-beverly-hills.

4   E. F. Romero, "They Wonder How We Do It': Downey Unified—a School District in LA's Shadow with the Same Student Demographics—Is Getting 96% of Kids Across the Graduation Stage," *LA School Report*, February 6, 2017, http://laschoolreport.com/they-wonder-how-we-do-it-downey-unified-a-school-district-in-las-shadow-with-the-same-student-demographics-is-getting-96-of-kids-across-the-graduation-stage/.

5   E. F. Romero, "'They Wonder How We Do It.'"

6   "About the 21st Century Learning Exemplar Program," P21: Partnership for 21st Century Learning, 2017, http://www.p21.org/exemplar-program-case-studies/about-the-program.

7   J. Robin, "PME: My Advice to You." *UnBoxed* 1 (Spring 2008).

8   R. Berger, L. Rugen, and L. Woodfin, "Celebrations of Learning," *Leaders of Their Own Learning* (San Francisco, CA: Jossey-Bass, 2014).

Tammy Reina, North County Tecnology Academy

176   *Inspiration, Not Replication*

Transforming Students and Teachers:
Building Capacity for Project-Based Learning in Juvenile Court & Community Schools

Lillian Hsu
High Tech High

In the fall of 2015, Tammy Reina found herself confronted with the most difficult year of teaching she had experienced in her 18 years as an educator. Tammy teaches English Language Arts at the North County Technology Academy, a juvenile court and community school in San Marcos, California. Her specific school site—encompassing roughly 30 students and three teachers—serves young men and women in grades six to 12 who have been expelled from their district school or who are on probation. Tammy's students rotate in and out of the program constantly. Over the span of a semester, she regularly experiences 50 to 70% turnover of students in her classroom. North County Technology Academy also faces the unique challenge of being one of the only sites in North County that accepts middle school students who have been expelled. Tammy says:

It's a challenging age. They're caught between wanting to impress peers and wanting to engage in academia. What we had last year was about 15 to 20 middle schoolers that had all been expelled and pretty much from the same school. They came in, and they just took over our program. It was really hard. We were struggling as teachers...That really negative energy they were generating...they were moving that into all of our classrooms.

Tammy is a teacher with Momentum Learning. Formerly known as the Juvenile Court and Community Schools (JCCS), Momentum Learning serves 3,170 youth in the juvenile justice system, aged ten to 21. Their schools, numbering 24 in total, span San Diego County, from San Ysidro in the south to San Marcos in the north. Many of Momentum's students have been expelled from their district schools, incarcerated, or placed on probation. Others are homeless youth, foster children, youth with severe mental health issues, or youth who have been trafficked or detained. Many are gang-affiliated, subject to California's controversial gang enhancement laws. The students Momentum Learning serves are arguably some of San Diego's most traumatized and marginalized young people.

Equipped with a strong desire to help young people create positive change in their lives, Tammy started out her career as a probation officer in the maximum security unit of San Diego County's juvenile hall. After witnessing the tremendous impact that juvenile court school teachers had on their students, Tammy enrolled in a teacher credentialing program and began teaching with Momentum Learning, a step that she describes as "truly one of the best decisions of my life."

But this past year was unusually challenging. Tammy

explains:

> We were really struggling in terms of culture
> in my program. Student culture. Our kids
> come from all over North County, from a
> whole lot of different gangs. But as much or
> more importantly, they're just struggling with
> so much. A high percentage of the kids are in
> crisis. And academics aren't at the forefront.
> That's not the pressing need in their lives.

Tammy recounts that eighteen months later, student
culture at her school has transformed utterly.

> Just between last year and this year, it is not
> even the same program. I think project-based
> learning has had a whole lot to do with that.
> Restorative practices have had a lot to do with
> that.... Everything kind of came into alignment.

On a recent evening in March 2017, at a town hall event
staged in the school's communications lab, Tammy's
students stood tall in front of their parents, educators,
and local community members. Their voices grew
increasingly confident as they took turns moderating a
community panel about what society needs to provide
young people to keep them from turning to gangs. Earlier
in the evening, as part of their project exhibition, the
students had shared their science posters depicting the
impact of violence on brain health, as well as their cause
and solution essays on gang violence. For the panel, the
students had invited four dynamic community experts:
Reginald Washington, founder of the emotional literacy
program, Project A.W.A.R.E.; San Diego County Office
of Education Interim Superintendent Edward Velasquez;
probation officer Donna Scimo; and former gang member
turned artist-activist Saul Figueroa, whose beautiful
mural Tammy had admired every day when she was a

probation officer at juvenile hall.

After watching several recordings of CNN town halls and dissecting the physical configuration of the events, the composition of the panels, and the way questions were framed, Tammy's students designed every element of their own town hall. They brainstormed questions for the panelists around three themes—Stories, Causes, and Solutions—and they set up audio and video equipment to capture the panelists' responses for a documentary. Even though they had done multiple dress rehearsals, the students were anxious. "The idea that they were running something and in charge of something, that they would be speaking to a relatively large audience...the kids were nervous, really nervous."

By Tammy's account they need not have worried.

> The town hall was two hours, and it could have gone four. It was a huge, huge success. The kids had to stand there for two hours and maintain their composure. The room filled up. But no one backed out. They did a fantastic job. This doesn't just happen. [It takes] a whole lot of time. A whole lot of space. A whole lot of resources. Human resources.

Those resources began to take shape when Tammy joined the Project-Based Learning pilot within Momentum Learning.

Thematic, Interdisciplinary Project-Based Learning: Origins

In July 2015, Sean Morrill, Senior Director for the San Diego County Office of Education, hired Matt Simon to lead the Project-Based Learning pilot at Momentum Learning. Participation in the Career Pathways PBL

Leadership Academy in 2016-17 as a grantee of the California Career Pathways Trust complemented internal leadership from Sean, Matt, and others. Prior to joining Momentum, Matt taught eleventh and twelfth grade humanities at High Tech High Chula Vista, a project-based learning (PBL) school in south San Diego County. Following the murder of a classmate and the massacres in Aurora, Oak Creek, and Newtown, Matt and his biology teaching partner, Nuvia Ruland, designed an interdisciplinary project that engaged their team of 45 students in producing a documentary called Beyond the Crossfire. Over the course of two years, Matt, Nuvia, and their students traveled across the country, investigating what young people could do to reduce the amount of gun violence in the United States.

Research for the documentary led the students to Los Angeles County Office of Education's Road to Success Academy (RTSA). Matt and a small team traveled to Saugus, California, to visit a school serving young women detained at Camp Scott-Scudder. There they conducted extensive interviews with RTSA Director, Diana Velasquez-Campos, who had pioneered a new model of instruction and intervention for incarcerated youth, a framework she called Thematic, Interdisciplinary Project-Based Learning (TIP).

Diana explains her vision for Road to Success Academy in the documentary.

> The themes were a way to bring about that social-emotional connection and to tie that into what we were doing. So here we have themes where we are addressing things like self-esteem, we're addressing things like hope, self-empowerment. And it's the cycle that we want to see the girls go through to then leave us and begin a new life. And interdisciplinary

Matt Simon, Momentum Learning

Inspiration, Not Replication

was important because you have to be able to go deep with this content...I remember sharing with a colleague when we were starting: What I want to do is create a private school within a juvenile detention facility. I want kids outside of this facility not to want to come in, but to say, "I hear that school is awesome. I wish I could go into that school.'"

Filming the documentary also took Matt's team to the San Diego Juvenile Court and Community Schools, where High Tech High Chula Vista senior Ciera Ybarra interviewed Sean Morrill. During this interview, Sean committed to visiting RTSA in Los Angeles. He not only followed through on this promise; he also brought with him a crew of teachers and instructional coaches from Momentum. After two visits, Sean made the decision to pilot this work in San Diego and recruited Matt to take on the challenge of leading the program. Describing the impact of these visits, Matt says:

> The greatest catalyzing force was teachers seeing PBL in a court school setting in L.A.... It's a game-changer when you're like, PBL, PBL, PBL. Wait, there's someone doing this with court school students? That is very different than doing it in a charter school or very different than even doing it in a comprehensive school, for our teachers. Our teachers truly believe we have a unique situation, and we do. So RTSA doing what they're doing is big in terms of opening up possibilities.

Matt adapted RTSA's model to create a revised TIP framework for Momentum Learning, describing the three core elements as:

- THEMATIC: Teachers, students, and community partners engage in discussion to determine what character strengths students most need to be successful.
- INTERDISCIPLINARY: Teachers, students, and community partners engage in discussion to determine which meaningful and relevant interdisciplinary topic students will explore through the lens of each theme.
- PROJECT-BASED: Students demonstrate their content learning, literary skill development, and 21st century skill development through authentic, high-quality projects they design, refine, and exhibit to a real audience who may ask questions.

Beginning with Dialogue

When Matt joined the organization, he found that teachers within Momentum Learning, like teachers in most settings, faced the challenge of navigating multiple initiatives—balancing disparate, sometimes competing strands of work that they felt obligated to master in their practice. Matt quickly recognized that PBL would be "best positioned, not as another initiative, but as the piece that can let all initiatives find their voice."

In describing the pilot to teachers at Momentum, he framed TIP as a vehicle for bringing together arts integration, pathways to college, community connections, counseling, and literacy. "It's the framework that helps adults collaborate for the sake of the kids," says Matt.

A former community organizer turned educator, Matt has a gift for facilitating tough conversations and for helping folks with widely differing perspectives find common ground. He applied these skills to his new role at Momentum Learning. He advises:

Every conversation you have needs to be

about kids, about making choices that are best for kids. This has a way of causing people to let go of the things preventing them from taking risks. When people look at education differently, suddenly they are willing to make radical instructional shifts.

Unsurprisingly, then, the first step in Momentum Learning's TIP framework is dialogue. Matt describes this foundational step as "a discussion, honest, robust, and often lengthy, between teachers, community partners, and ideally the students themselves."

During the discussion, these key stakeholders wrestle in earnest with the following questions:

- Who are our students?
  - What are their strengths?
  - What have they overcome? What are they still overcoming?
- What are our greatest hopes for our students' future success?
  - What do we want for our students when they are adults...when they are 30...40...50...?
- What do our students need to achieve real, deep, lasting success?
  - What skills will our students need again and again to achieve and sustain this success?
  - What character strengths will our students need again and again to achieve and sustain this success?

These discussions are often challenging to facilitate, as they strike at individuals' core beliefs about kids, education, and equity. Matt's strong knowledge of restorative practices and his skill at engaging participants in circles have served him well in guiding these conversations. "The importance of candor and not taking anything personally" is another foundational tenet of productive

Valentin Escanuela, Momentum Learning

Inspiration, Not Replication

dialogue, as well as "leaving the power to decide with the teachers."

Thematic

Teachers at each Momentum site make the decision following these initial conversations whether to move toward project-based learning. If they do, the next step is to generate a "Cycle of Themes" focused on cultivating specific character strengths within their students. An example of the character strengths embedded within a Cycle of Themes comes from Road to Success camps Gonzales and Miller:

> Our vision is to guide our students through the process of **self-discovery**, leading them to develop a vision for their future and to pursue that vision with **courage**. By examining their true nature of courage, students will learn to align their actions, words, and deeds with their vision to become men of integrity. Men of **integrity** are **socially responsible** leaders in their communities who reflect on their actions and their impact on their communities.

Valentin Escanuela, a vice-principal with Momentum Learning, attests to the value of focusing on character strengths as a core element of TIP.

> The reason why I'm such a big proponent of Thematic Interdisciplinary Project-Based Learning is because our kids need a little bit more than your traditional student. Obviously, they haven't had a whole lot of success in traditional school. We needed to find a way to engage kids back into their learning and to school and help them learn 1) that they can be successful and 2) important skills that they will

take with them after they leave our programs. TIP gave us that tool and that framework to be able to do that for our students.

Valentin oversees six schools in the Momentum network, including a pregnant and parent teen program in San Ysidro, three community schools, and two juvenile court schools. After visiting Road to Success Academy in Los Angeles, he became convinced that TIP's focus on character strengths would meet the needs of his students' specific life circumstances. Rather than sharing one set of character strengths across all of Momentum Learning, Escanuela speaks to the power of personalizing the character strengths to the needs of students at each individual school.

> Every site is different. Every site has different needs. And the themes were created by the people that work closest to the kids. Probation officers were involved in the meetings. We've had students involved in the meetings. We had teachers, counselors. So anybody who works closest to the kids is coming together to really talk about it and have conversations like: "What are some things we are seeing in our students that we can address as a whole and be thematic with our approach?"

Interdisciplinary Project-Based Learning

After designing a Cycle of Themes, teachers, community partners and ideally the students themselves engage in more discussion around the following questions:

- What meaningful, interdisciplinary topic will our students explore through the lens of each theme?
  - What academic content will students learn through the lens of each interdisciplinary topic and theme?

- What will students read, write, and speak about to develop expertise on the topic/theme/content?
- What projects will students design, refine, and exhibit to an audience to demonstrate their expertise?
- What skills will students develop, practice, and demonstrate over the course of their learning and work?

Matt's emphasis on bringing students into these discussions is what attracted Tammy Reina to the TIP pilot.

> What really appealed to me about it was the idea that there would be student voice and choice in the selection of the topic. Through choosing topics and the learning that was very relevant to them, I started to see signs of engagement, I started to see buy-in, I started to see students caring about what they produced.

She appreciated the way Matt modeled deep respect for student voice in these discussions.

> We were still working really hard to create an academic culture. We weren't there yet. And Matt just brings this air of seriousness but belief in them, and the kids respond to it. The way he had with our students...I mean he immediately connected with some students and was building them up in terms of their writing and their self-efficacy. And it was just kind of instantaneous.

Tammy believes that Matt's commitment to treating students with respect and demonstrating belief in their highest potential was key in creating buy-in for the pilot. Matt agrees. "The desire to do right by kids and a deep belief in kids is at the core of this work."

Juvenile Justice: The Broader Context

In the United States, the foundation underlying the creation of a separate juvenile justice system is the principle of parens patriae, the idea that the state can act as a parent when a young person commits a petty or serious crime, or when he or she violates age-based societal norms by committing "status offenses," acts such as purchasing alcohol that are considered a law violation only because of a youth's status as a minor. In these circumstances, the state steps in and assumes the role of protector, caretaker, and disciplinarian. The juvenile justice system takes in some of the most vulnerable young people in our society and commits, ostensibly, to providing these youth with rehabilitation, education, and preparation for the future.

According to a 2016 report produced by the Youth Law Center, a public interest law firm that works to protect children in the nation's foster care and justice systems from abuse or neglect, 85% of juvenile court school students are youth of color. While African-American students make up only 6% of California's total enrollment, they are the most overrepresented group in the juvenile court schools with 20.6% of court school enrollment. Latino students make up 53.6% of total state enrollment and represent 61.4% of court school enrollment. Thus, the report underscores, "to talk about the juvenile justice system's educational failures and missed opportunities is to talk about a systemic neglect of a largely Black and Latino community and a perpetuation and exacerbation of the inequality that beget such disparities."

In 2014, the Youth Law Center reports, 47,655 California youth spent some part of their school year in a juvenile court school. Many of these young people entered the system with significant educational challenges. Two out of five youth in juvenile court schools come from homes where a language other than English is dominant, and 27.5% are classified as English Language Learners. Nationally, between 30% and 50% qualify for special education services. Most strikingly, the vast majority of youth in the juvenile justice system have experienced one or more forms of trauma, which can significantly disrupt concentration and interfere with other aspects of learning.

In order to gauge the academic progress of youth while in custody, court schools receiving Title I funding are required by federal law to assess reading and math proficiency for long-term students upon entry to and exit from juvenile detention facilities. Twenty-nine percent of California court students tested demonstrated a loss in reading ability during their period of incarceration, while 27.7% exhibited diminished math skills. These percentages are likely artificially low because the schools failed to assess nearly 60% of the youth served.

The latest data shows that upon exiting court schools, only 56% of students enroll in their local school district within 30 to 90 days. For 2013-14, California's court schools had a dropout rate of 37.7%, compared to an adjusted statewide rate of 11.6%. Ten counties in California had court schools with dropout rates of 60% or higher, and another five had rates between 40% and 59%.

In light of this and other troubling data detailed in their report, the Youth Law Center calls for juvenile court schools to develop more effective strategies for engaging their students and for supporting students with the skills and guidance they need to pursue further education.

Jackie Smith, Girls' Rehabilitation Facility

Inspiration, Not Replication

The Pilot: School Visits in Boston

Along with Tammy Reina, Jackie Smith was one of the teachers who took part in the pilot. Jackie teaches History and Math at Girls' Rehabilitation Facility (GRF), a juvenile court school that serves up to 30 incarcerated girls between the ages of 13 and 17. During her college years, Jackie took a series of courses that inspired a strong desire to work with young people who had been overlooked by society. Though she had originally planned on becoming a social worker, Jackie ultimately decided she could make a bigger impact on young people by teaching because she saw education as a gateway to so many opportunities.

In fall 2015, the Momentum leadership team organized a teacher study trip to Massachusetts, a challenging travel experience designed to give the pilot teachers an opportunity to observe innovative teaching and learning in action at eight different schools in the greater Boston area.

"The Boston trip was life-changing professionally," says Jackie. "Seeing the inequity that occurs across the country. Being plucked out of your district, seeing something with completely fresh eyes, I got to see what was working and what wasn't."

Jackie's most memorable learning came at Rivers and Revolutions, a school within a school in the affluent community of Concord, Massachusetts. Fifty juniors and seniors within Concord-Carlisle High School come together with five teachers for a semester to study essential concepts and questions organized around four interdisciplinary units of study: rivers and revolutions, air and fire, love and journey, and equilibrium. Students engage in fieldwork, exploring nature and cultural settings within the community, and complete an investigation presented through artifact and writing. "We are either in the mud outside, at a museum, in Boston, or wherever the wind takes us," one of the students told the visiting group.

Jackie was struck by how much Rivers and Revolutions' well-funded facilities resembled a college campus. Even more strikingly, she observed how much the students at Rivers and Revolutions interacted with the independence and poise of college students.

> I felt like the students really took ownership of their learning. I felt like I was in a college class, where the teacher didn't have to prompt the students to share what they had learned. They were able to form their own groups and have discussions and then present their work, and it was as if the teacher was able to just stand there and watch all this beautiful choreography take place without directing it. The students were able to take ownership over everything they had done. To me that was amazing.

At the same time, Jackie was struck by the startlingly different demographics she observed at Rivers and Revolutions compared to the demographics of the students at Momentum Learning.

> To be completely frank, what I then found troubling, was when I looked all around, it was predominantly white students. I was taken aback by the inequity of the situation. I teach predominantly Latino and African American and Asian students.... I want all of my students to have that kind of education and this chance. I want to see all of my kids out on that field, [more] than just the couple of them that get bussed in. I just had this complete awakening

as an educator. Why can't my kids who don't look like these kids achieve and have the same opportunities?

This contrast was particularly striking when the Momentum team followed up their visit to Rivers and Revolutions with visits to Boston schools that had a more similar demographic to their own. Matt added:

> We went to a court school, where it was like a shell game. They kept moving us from place to place, we just couldn't see any kids learning. We finally get to a place where kids are learning and the kids are basically drawing pictures.... Then we went to another place that was just serving purely our kind of kids, like an alternative school, and it was a mess. Tons and tons of kids were getting kicked out of class, or placed on timeouts. So we just kept having this experience where we'd go to this genius amazing school for really rich kids, and then we'd go to a school for kids of color or kids with low socioeconomic status. And we just saw the gap.

The pilot team returned to San Diego with fire in their bellies, intent on taking action. As Matt reflects:

> It was galvanizing for us in terms of equity, and it was also galvanizing for us in terms of teachers could really dream big. I remember my summary statement at the end was basically: All of you, you are visionaries. You have a very powerful vision for what you want to do with your students, and let's do that. Let's figure out how to make this happen.

The Pilot: Working Toward a First Exhibition

The teachers began the pilot a week after returning from Boston. Bringing together a group of 12 teachers from six Momentum Learning schools, Matt hosted a day-long professional learning workshop where they began to imagine what a very small exhibition might look like. Matt had initially envisioned that the pilot group would study PBL for one trimester; design a project second trimester; and launch, facilitate, and exhibit the project by third trimester. But a subset of the pilot teachers, specifically, the team from Reflections Central School in La Mesa, wanted to jump in immediately. Matt recalls:

> They came to me after the first professional learning on PBL and were like, "We want to start Monday." This was like a Friday. "We want to start this next week.... We all know this is good for kids, we all know this is better than what we are currently doing, so we're just going to go for it."

The Transformative Power of Exhibitions

Cindy Stallo, a special education teacher from Reflections Central, was part of this pioneering crew that jumped headfirst into PBL. Her very first project was an exploration of spoken word, where students wrote narrative pieces about their lives and then turned them into slam poetry to perform in front of an audience.

Cindy's commitment to exhibiting her students' work publicly turned out to be a powerful catalyst for generating student and teacher engagement with project-based learning. Matt, who coached both the students and the teachers throughout this project, recalls the explosive power of their final performances.

The kids just blew the doors off of their exhibition. Probation was there and were saying things like, "We've been working in this district for 15 to 25 years; we've never seen anything like this. We seriously thought everyone was crazy. After a few days, we started to relax our rules because the kids seemed like they had more purpose. By the end of this, we totally threw away our rules because the kids were running everywhere, but they were running with such purpose. These poems, these projects blew us away. How do we do more of this?

Stacy Spector, Momentum Learning's Executive Director at this time, was in the audience. Matt recalls, "[Stacy] stood up and said, 'When probation is saying, I've been working in this district for 20 years and I've never ever seen anything this powerful from our kids and from our teachers, you know we are moving in the right direction.'"

Stacy invited all of Cindy's students to present their spoken word performance on stage at a town hall meeting at the University of San Diego in front of all 300 or so Momentum Learning staff. This event was a turning point for the organization, catalyzing many teachers across the network to sit up and express interest in PBL. Matt explains:

A lot of staff members in that audience were like, "I decided I was going to give it a shot or at least learn more about this when I saw those kids.... I know those kids, I've worked with those kids. And oh my gosh, I want to do that." Plus a lot of other people have said they were even more struck by more than the slam poetry itself, just the way the kids supported each other. Like a kid getting really nervous and a bunch of the students being like, "We got

Cindy Stallo, Reflections

Inspiration, Not Replication

you. You can do this." That camaraderie, that was really, really powerful. To watch one kid after the next do that, it really had a disarming impact and brought folks back to the kids and to the learning. Our pilot grew a lot after that in terms of the total number of people.

This transformative moment for the adults in the organization was similarly transformative for the students. The exhibition was a life-changing event for Reflections student Nasim, who had been with Cindy since the age of 13. As Cindy explains:

Nasim was pretty gregarious already, just not engaged a lot in school. He had a lot of stuff going on on the outside. But he got so focused on this project. [At the exhibition] Nasim not only did his poetry, but he emceed it, just kind of made everything happen.

Nasim's self-esteem skyrocketed as a result of this experience.

The confidence he has, he has been different ever since then.... He really just stayed motivated in school, he got some notoriety, he kind of became a peer with the adults. He became the expert, and that's really changed his relationship with a lot of staff and adults. I think he felt really a part of the process, and he felt important.

Now 17, Nasim graduated from high school in March 2017, an achievement Cindy attributes to the transformative impact of PBL. Cindy continues:

I think that translates to all of the kids. I get a lot less in my classroom now: "Why are we learning this? What's this going to do for my life?" The kids feel like so much a bigger part in partnering with us and also co-creating the curriculum. Seeing themselves as more of an expert on something really raises their self-esteem. That praise from outside adults has been the biggest thing I've been able to see with my own eyes.

Sometimes they don't realize 'til the day of exhibition that other people besides me were going to listen, even though I tell them. When people show up and they have to present to another adult, something clicks and everything comes together for them. It's like a magical wand.

Tammy Reina echoes Cindy's observations. "The fact that the community and people would be there to see what they had done, that was really important to them."

Tammy's first mini project, entitled "Weathering the Storm," engaged her students in exploring the theme of resilience. Her students met with oceanographers from University of California San Diego and investigated what an El Nino might do to their North County community. Their first exhibition was a modest one. Tammy recalls, "As far as the exhibition goes, it was really limited, and kids were kind of in and out of it. It was our first attempt at it. It was rough around the edges."

Out of their 30 or so students, Tammy noted that only ten or 12 had actively engaged in the project and created a product that they felt comfortable displaying publicly. However, she felt compelled to find ways to include all 30 students in the public exhibition.

She reflects,

> Matt's a firm believer in you don't ever shame a kid that didn't really engage in the project. So we had to find roles for those kids to engage in on exhibition day because they really hadn't completed the work. So that was a struggle.

But the struggle resulted in significant dividends. Tammy describes the transformative power of that first exhibition in enlarging both teachers' and students' sense of possibility:

> Of course, all the teachers that are doing this, walk into these exhibitions so anxious. We're like: "This is going to explode, oh my god, this isn't going to happen. This isn't going to come together." And then it happens, and it comes together more beautifully than you could have possibly imagined. We do a lot of reflecting afterwards, and the kids that really had engaged felt so good about what they had done. The next day, even though maybe a third of our students had really participated in it, there was this incredible feel good quality about what had happened, and that creates more buy-in with more students.

The positive reflections generated from the first exhibition motivated more students to engage actively with the second project. "So our second exhibition, which was about issues in society, we had virtually the entire program ready to stand up and exhibit their work and talk about their learning, and that growth was absolutely incredibly insane."

Student Engagement, Teacher Engagement

Tammy believes that witnessing students' engagement with learning deepen and grow is the most powerful catalyst for generating teacher investment in PBL. "For me the biggest thing is the student engagement.... The buy-in comes from the engagement, not just of the kids but of the teachers as well."

Valentin agrees. His strategy for getting staff on board with PBL focused on having teachers share their stories and their learning with their colleagues. Inviting teachers to attend exhibitions, to see the powerful work kids were producing, ignited excitement among teachers and created openness to considering new ways of expanding their practice.

> I've been with the organization for 12 years, and this is probably the most enthusiasm I have ever seen in teachers since I've been with the organization as far as the work, the kind of projects they're doing, the kind of work that's happening in the classrooms, the kind of ideas that teachers are just coming up with, and being real creative with their practice, and their passion of what they want to teach kids and want kids to learn. Teachers see that and it's contagious, right? When you start seeing success at one site, you start seeing what kids are doing at one site, it kind of transitions to the other site. Like, "I want to do that, I want to do that. What are you guys doing? I want to do what you're doing."

Supports Teachers Need to Make the Shift

"Once you have that interest and that hunger, people want to know, how do you do this?" asks Matt. His approach to supporting Momentum teachers in the transition to PBL, begins with making the goals simple and clear. He breaks down his aspirations for PBL at Momentum in this way:

> [You want students to] develop a deep understanding of something. And if you're going to learn something with real legitimate depth, you've got to read a ton and you've got to get some experiences and you've got to talk about it, and then you have to demonstrate that deep understanding through a project that gets refined for an audience.

Demystifying the complexities of PBL and making its strategies and methods accessible is key.

> So much of it is about comprehensible input. How do you take something that is actually really complex and simplify it in a way that teachers are like, "I got it!" And then the next project, they're like, "Wait a minute. I don't know if I had it before, but now I really got it." You just add another dimension each [time] as they get deeper into it.

Over the past two years, Matt has invested a significant amount of time to create differentiated planning tools. "We are working with 50 different teachers, and everyone plans differently and everyone needs something a little different to where they are," says Matt. "Meeting somebody where they are and differentiating a little bit is how you do it."

Tammy has found Matt's personalized support and guidance invaluable.

> He was there every step along the way. When

we needed to tweak something and when the kids seemed to be losing interest or their interest was waning, he would always be there to find a way to pull the kids back together. Or if we needed to modify the scope of the project, he was there to help me figure [it] out."

Tammy explains that a relentless belief in every teacher's potential to grow and change lies at the core of Matt's commitment to meeting the needs of each individual.

That's something about him I've appreciated so much. We have some teachers that are really stellar, and they shine. And we have other teachers that struggle, and that's true in any district. And I've never heard him berate a teacher. He speaks to the challenging circumstances within which we teach, and he focuses on growth: teacher growth, student growth, program growth. And we need that. We really do need that.

In approaching his work, Matt sees a parallel between the students and the teachers.

One of the things I find myself talking about a lot is that all of our students have enormous amounts of under-developed or untapped potential. Our job is to develop that potential. I see our teachers the same way. They all have high potential, and we haven't done enough to develop it with many of our teachers.

To activate that potential, Matt maximizes every professional learning opportunity he has with teachers, modeling, at every step, the kind of deep reading, writing, thinking, and speaking he wants to see in the project-based lessons teachers design.

Literacy-Rich PBL

Matt describes his aspirations for instruction at Momentum as "literacy rich PBL," in large part because of the students the organization serves.

> You look at our district, and there's a substantial number of language learners, there's a substantial number of students who just have massive holes in their transcripts. Students who from probably kindergarten forward were the kids who were told, you have too much energy or you're being defiant. Here's your little packet. You can go work in the corner, and the packet...it's not going to require a lot of thinking. So you have kids who somehow are progressing through the education system at large, not just necessarily our system, who have major gaps in terms of literacy.

Matt firmly believes that lifting literacy and language development within the context of PBL is crucial to support court and community school students in their path toward college and career.

> You are not going to get very far if you cannot read at a high level and if you cannot communicate your ideas through writing. I truly believe you are setting up kids with a false sense of hope if you push college and you don't have them reading and writing at a college level. And there are a lot of things that go into being career ready. Working with others is vital. But if you're a strong communicator... you can open some doors for yourself. You can get that interview in a way that you could have somebody who is just as thoughtful, just as sweet, just as bright, but they struggle with

oral and written communication, they're not going to go as far. It really was like,"Who are our kids? And let's meet their needs."

In framing the stages of PBL for the TIP framework, Matt explicitly called out Developing Deep Understanding, describing it as:

> Here students develop expertise on the essential question as well as the specific content topic and/or problem, primarily through reading (learning from texts) and hands-on experiences (learning by doing) accompanied by a steady dose of thinking, writing, and discussing what's being learned.

This inquiry cycle of reading, writing, and speaking is central to the literacy-rich PBL practices that Matt models for his teachers. In creating this cycle, Matt drew inspiration from the work of Ron Berger on transformational literacy, as well as the work of Gloria Ladson-Billings and Jeff Duncan Andrade on culturally relevant pedagogy.

> [When you're taught mostly] through lecture or through powerpoint, or through a teacher summarizing stuff for you, one, you're not growing your own reading ability, but you're also not really learning it for yourself. You're not thinking. You're just taking in information.

Instead, Matt believes:

> Let the text be the teacher. Thoughtfully select texts, and have kids really learn from them, but not just summarize them, really think critically about them. How do you do that without engaging in conversations with others?...so

this cycle of reading and thinking and talking leads to better writing. Or reading and writing and thinking leads to better talking. It's this continuous loop.

Jackie Smith attests to the power of introducing thoughtfully selected texts in the context of an engaging project.

> You are not just giving your kids something to read without a purpose. You have to choose your readings very intentionally. When you do that, the kids home into it. They're like: "Okay, this is why we're reading this." The good thing about PBL too is that things that you don't initially think may come out of that reading, the kids really make a connection.

Digging deeply into meaningful texts, in turn, inspires powerful writing.

> When it then comes to the writing, the kids have this itch: I've got to get everything that I've learned into this essay. It makes the writing component easier because the kids are really invested into the subject.... And revision is so key because you're presenting your work to your peers, your teachers, people of the community. The kids have this intrinsic motivation to put their best work forward because they know all these people are going to be listening, reading, asking them questions about it.

Jackie leverages student-centered discussion as a key strategy within the inquiry cycle. Her motivation for this approach reaches all the way back to her visit to Rivers and Revolutions.

It honestly came from that Boston trip. If those kids could do that, my kids could do it. I just have to restructure my way of teaching, my way of thinking. For you and I, inherently we do that when we read an article, just as educators. We take for granted that our kids are going to do that, when they need to be taught that.

Within every project, Jackie creates multiple opportunities for students to engage in conversation protocols, especially fishbowl discussions, with an outer circle listening as an inner circle speaks. "That way the students have to not only speak about a topic but they also have to listen and critique their peers on a topic, which sometimes I think is more powerful than just talking."

Tammy Reina points to two specific students who have been transformed by literacy-rich PBL practices.

I've got a Sean who's a special education student. Has never shone in a traditional classroom, ever, has never felt exemplary. And his friend Carlos. And they both really, really struggle academically. But they're there every single day. And they're staying with us as we read these passages. When they write in their journals...these particular kids have just been pushing themselves, pushing themselves in terms of their writing. And they stood up and they talked about ISIS in our last presentation. It was kind of a muddled presentation and it wasn't all that clear, but they worked with it, and they revised it, and they refined it. They were the group where we said, if you can memorize what's on your notes, it's better to hold your notes down at your sleeve and just to speak. And they took that to heart, and they memorized everything they were going to present.

Carlos definitely holds an IEP, specific learning disability, has a very difficult time articulating his thoughts. But he's pulling himself together so much.... He volunteers to read even though he muddles through the reading, he struggles with that.... Carlos has started to not only see himself as a leader, but he's really cool when another kid is struggling with something by throwing a comment in there, "That's okay, I've struggled." You can tell he is feeling as though he's leading the class, as opposed to being the one in the back corner.

Depth of Ownership, Depth of Thought

Now, in the thick of her fourth project, Tammy is excited about the depth of ownership and depth of thought that she sees emerging from her students. At the beginning of this project, Tammy once again engaged her students in brainstorming societal topics that felt relevant to them. On one whiteboard, students brainstormed around the question of "What do you want to learn?" On the second board, they brainstormed responses to: "How are we going to exhibit our work? What will the product be at the end?"

As a result of their brainstorming session, the students chose gang violence, causes and solutions, as the topic they most wanted to investigate. For their products, students decided to create a documentary and design T-shirts that communicated key learnings from their research.

In English class, Tammy's students read extensively on the topic, digging into Luis Rodriguez's memoir, Always Running, as well as Dr. Victor Rios' texts, Punished: Policing the Lives of Black and Latino Boys and Street

Life: Poverty, Gangs, and a Ph.D. As they unpacked these complex texts, students considered what was happening in these young men's lives that led them to join a gang. They also thought deeply about what society lacks. What was society not providing these kids that they needed?

By contrasting the communities where they saw gang violence with those in which they did not, the students identified affluence and poverty as a clear dividing line. But the students probed even deeper. Tammy elaborates:

> We've gotten into some really cool passages where Luis [Rodriguez] would say, "We created a thread out of nothing. We didn't have Boy Scouts. We didn't have this. Schools pushed us out the doors, didn't treat us with dignity and respect. We had none of these things. We originally started creating these cliques because we wanted a group to go to the beach on Saturdays. Because we wanted to go camping. Because we had a group that liked to play baseball. So these gangs kind of began out of a group of young men who had a common purpose that really wanted to do something prosocial. But nothing was happening in society to meet those needs."

Drawing parallels between their own lives and the lives of the subjects they studied, Tammy's students had an insight.

> We talked about how those cliques moved from prosocial to really becoming more formalized gangs where they're adopting colors and engaging in criminal activity. And what we homed in on was the idea that there weren't any adults supervising these groups. So whereas you'll have a group of Boy Scouts,

same purpose, and these boys grow up to become young upstanding men in society going off to college. ...there was some mentorship there that didn't happen with these boys. So we've homed in on that.

After the town hall event, Tammy's students have turned their attention to completing the documentary. Working in two crews, the students spend at least one day a week doing formal videotaped interviews or driving around their local community gathering B roll (footage used to complement the interview). In a few weeks, the students will be traveling to Los Angeles to film an interview with author Luis Rodriguez.

Tammy believes that PBL has engaged her students more deeply in critical thinking than ever before. Indeed, their aspiration for the documentary they are producing is to challenge and dispel commonly held misconceptions about the young people in gangs.

So there are those that would argue you are not hitting every single standard. We feel the pushback on that mostly from history teachers that feel tied to a chronological period of time because you're not going to cover the breadth of history in project-based learning. But my perspective, and those that have engaged in the work, is that we're looking at new standards. And now we are looking at standards of thought as opposed to standards of content necessarily.

Tammy points to her student Amado as an example of a someone who has thrived on the critical thinking facilitated by PBL.

When we took on our topics, our community issues last project, he took on the idea of racism in society. And it began with the idea that the really explicit racism we saw back in the 30s, 40s, pre-civil rights era, you think that that's gone away, but then he contrasted it with the examples of unarmed black men being shot, and it was just a beautiful kind of pulling together of the ideas. And his thoughts were so deep and he continues to go deep as we're doing this project now. When I asked him why he had chosen gangs, causes and solutions [for our current project], he said, "Because it's a very complex topic. Because there's not just one answer." So I love that about him.

At the end of last year, all of the English Language Arts teachers in the TIP pilot came together and pulled out the state standards, checking to see whether their kids were beginning, intermediate, or proficient in each one. Tammy reflects:

> And we had hit on pretty much every single standard in the work we had done! And not intentionally. That was a big kind of shift for us. You don't begin with the standards in mind because that will kill any love, any enthusiasm for what's going on in the classroom. By default, our kids are hitting the standards, in terms of thinking, in terms of writing, in terms of speaking. They're doing it.

Matt agrees that one of the biggest hurdles in spreading PBL has been the battle over coverage and exposure. When these concerns arise, he sits down with teachers to look deeply at the new standards to challenge misconceptions about what they truly ask of students. He engages teachers in dialogue around the following questions: "Which of these are most essential for our students to not only learn, but own for the rest of their lives? Are you teaching so kids are learning or so they are forgetting?" Most powerfully, he asks, "Who's this kid going to be in five years? Ten years?"

Changing Life Trajectories

At Reflections school, Cindy Stallo has witnessed the power of PBL in reshaping the trajectory of their lives. Her student, Elias, immediately comes to her mind. "Elias came to me six months ago, addicted to meth, smoking weed, depressed. He'd come in and put his head down in class. Nice kid but just not engaged at all."

The projects in Cindy's class began to reignite Elias's interest in learning.

> In December, we did our election project, and he did his on poverty. He researched a lot of what's going on with poverty in the U.S., mostly focusing on children and teens. But then he related it back to his family. So he interviewed his mom and his family to say, "Okay, here's the poverty line. Where do we stand?" Through it, he realized, "My family is in poverty. What can I do about that?" It became a really personal project for him.

She went on to describe the little speech Elias gave in December right before he graduated the program.

> His biggest thing in the speech was that when he came, he couldn't write an essay. He wouldn't have been able to read the things that we read and be able to understand them, and he said, "Now I can get up in front of adults and speak. I don't have a problem explaining what I'm doing." All of these things, he said, "It was all because of the work we did in PBL.

It was completely 100% based on that." The confidence and self-esteem I saw in that kid when he was leaving: it was a whole different person.

In January, Elias returned to El Cajon High, the school he had attended prior to Reflections. Cindy reported what he said about being there again and how his increased confidence has affected him beyond school:

> In the past he had never gone to school, gotten in fights, used drugs. I mean they kicked him out. So he went back in January. I talked to him after that, and he said that the teachers didn't even recognize him. He's going to be leading some peer groups. He doesn't even have any special ed support anymore. He went from almost complete special ed support to none. He said, "I know how to do my work. It's easy, and I get all my work done in class. It's all because of all the reading and writing you made me do."

> He's staying sober. He's participating in normal activities. He sees himself as a normal kid now. And I think so much of it is was the work we did, and he was only with me for a few months.... I wouldn't have thought that academics could help so much.

Next Steps for Momentum

From the initial pilot of 12 teachers from six schools, Momentum's PBL work has grown to more than 50 teachers in 16 schools. Now that the pilot has begun to bear fruit, significant questions about next steps have risen to the surface. Tammy says:

There's kind of this unspoken elephant. Do we continue along this road where it's a choice and teachers that choose to be involved in project-based learning thrive and those that choose not to are allowed to continue to choose whatever? Because we do believe in teacher choice. But if we identify this as a more effective, more engaging model for kids, is there a point where the district just says, "This is what we're doing. This is the model." And I have struggles around that. It would be my greatest hope that all teachers would see the value in what's going on, the enthusiasm around what's going on, not just from teachers but from students, and would be interested in jumping on board. But that's not a perfect world. So we do have a couple sites right now where PBL is being moved in, and there is some initial resistance.

Tammy believes that if the organization decides to go 100% PBL, a dramatic increase will be needed in support and teacher mentorship, including substantial attention to curriculum development.

One of the most beastly things of learning how to just jump in on this was pulling together the resources. There's no curriculum; you're creating your own. It's not so hard once you get the hang of it and you're pulling passages and you've got the right texts and you know where you're going. But when you don't, it's really kind of scary. It's a whole lot. So I guess I'd like to see something a little different for our new teachers...We've begun creating banks of projects for new teachers coming in, but there's a whole lot of training that has to be done with that.

In addition to providing more intensive support for new teachers, Tammy also feels that there is a continued need for differentiated support for all teachers pursuing PBL work.

> We need to feed the needs of new teachers coming into it, we need to feed the needs of intermediate teachers that have kind of been dabbling their feet but still need a great deal of support, and then we need to feed the needs of teachers that have been in it since the beginning and are ready to take it to the next level, which might be something like student portfolio assessment. There's something more that we could be doing. So it's this different level of support for teachers at different points.

Matt agrees that a deep investment in building teacher capacity is key in the continued growth of PBL across Momentum. For the 2017-2018 school year, he is working on assembling a strong team of coaches who have a depth of PBL experience to support other teachers in this work.

> We have to start with the teachers. The success of your students is first and foremost in their hands. Teachers, especially those who chose to work in this system, got into it for the purest of reasons. As a leader, your mission is to tap into that.

Matt constantly asks himself, "What are you doing to engage and excite teachers? Love on your teachers. You want your teachers to feel like your mission is to make them stars." Most importantly, as they continue to move forward, Matt holds to the belief that this work must be done through dialogue and collaboration. "Teachers need to feel that this is work done with them rather than done to them. Even if it's the most important work invented, people will resist if it's imposed on them."

PBL Alone Doesn't Fix Everything

While Tammy is a passionate advocate for the continued growth of PBL at Momentum, she is also emphatic that increased support for PBL alone will not address the immensity of need she sees with her students.

> While PBL does meet a whole lot of our kids' social and interpersonal needs, in the 20 years I've been teaching, I've never seen a population as a whole that is in the kind of crisis that I'm seeing our students in now. And that's through immigration reform. That's through homelessness. That's through mental illness. That's through all of these factors that are impacting their lives. For the past two, three months, we've had a major crisis in class at least once a week that's involved an ambulance or that's involved police intervention. A really serious crisis. And PBL doesn't fix that.

Tammy believes that in order for PBL to thrive across Momentum Learning, the organization needs to continue investing deeply in a combination of counseling and restorative practices. Unlike incarcerated students who have the stability of a residential facility, Tammy's community school students return home each night, which means contending with the gang activity and the drug usage in their neighborhoods.

> So as they're struggling with all of these crises in their lives, they're getting high. They're escaping, they're coping. So the level of kids showing up high each day…. How do we help them in all of the challenges they're going through in life, so that they can be in a place

where they can be open to something like PBL? Because while it does have that engaging factor, when a kid is getting kicked out of his apartment that day and his brother got arrested last night, I don't care how engaging the curriculum is. You've got a 50-50 chance of engaging him. You might engage him because it might be a distraction. But you might not. And if you can't, there should be something there to support that child. That isn't then taking the teacher away from what the teacher really needs to be doing with the rest of the students.

Matt agrees that PBL is not a cure-all. He advocates for more counselors, more administrators, and more staffing across Momentum, particularly at community sites like Tammy's that must contend with significant issues between rival gangs. Specifically, Matt would love to see an increase in the involvement of social workers, as well as the addition of Restorative Practice Ambassadors from the community who have the skills to de-escalate conflict and support Momentum students socio-emotionally.

With PBL at least our students can focus on problem solving and developing the skills they need to navigate the world of work and ideally college. But we are not going to make enough progress if we don't focus on the whole student and their basic needs—safety, shelter, psychological care.

Our Wildest Dreams

After doing this work intensely for the past two years, Matt continues to believe deeply that every student has the potential to be rehabilitated and can attain success. He is encouraged by the promising work happening with TIP at Momentum, but increasingly, he is also left with some big wonderings.

The messages that society is sending to our students is that they are throwaway kids. The forces being exerted on our students, the amount of trauma created on these young people.... As honorable as our work is, intervening at an earlier stage is very important. How do we work with kids before they end up in our system?

In an ideal world, Matt would be out of a job. There would be no more court and community schools because the larger system would more intentionally and more effectively provide all students with the supports they need to thrive in integrated schools, no matter the students' background, no matter the trauma that has touched their lives.

Cindy Stallo harbors her own wild dreams for the students and would-be students she teaches.

> For all of us in Momentum, because they come and go so much and because we have a short period of time with them, I can't imagine what more they would do if they had a full school day and three straight months without interruption. If my kids get caught using drugs, they go back to juvenile hall for three days, and then they come back. And then they go for two weeks and then they come back.... So there's not a lot of continuity in their placements. My dream would be, if I had the kids for a year, let's say...is that the kids could create something that would actually change their community.

Cindy describes a vision inspired by her former student, sixteen-year-old Julio.

> I have one student—he's not with me anymore,

he's been incarcerated. He lives in an area of town that I don't live in...and he is super gang-entrenched. That's his life, his uncle's life, his dad's life, his grandpa's life. Really, really addicted to drugs. Like he uses meth a lot, and that's when he has problems and goes away. When he came to me a year and a half ago, he was in one of our first TIP projects...The kids wrote a personal story about their lives, a personal narrative...and then they chose six words that really reflected that.... He wrote the first essay he's ever written in his whole life, and he's sixteen years old. After that process of that essay...his reflection was, "I can do school." Third or fourth grade reading level, very basic writing, but it was the first piece he had ever written.

The six word memoir says: "Just another kid in the streets." Because that's how he viewed himself, like I'm just another throwaway. But now I'm starting to see I can actually do something for myself.

For Julio's last project at Reflections, Cindy's students examined the presidential elections and its impact on our country and our world.

[They asked], 'Whoever gets elected, what are they actually going to do for me? Are they going to help my mom get a job? Are they going to pay my rent? Are they going to help me get off drugs? In reality no. So we started talking about what in our community is affecting us the most.

Julio focused his research on the American prison system, investigating the data on the number of people incarcerated and the disproportionate impact of the gang enhancement laws. His research and thinking led to an a-ha.

> What came out of this...was he told me, if kids in the hood could just get out and past their four corners and see what else is out there, they would have the motivation to change. It hit me so hard...He told the story about one guy who had gone to Utah, not even faraway, and he came back and showed pictures of the snowy mountains. And [Julio] was just like, "You can go there?" It was this idea of: "I can leave San Diego?" So he and I started talking about the idea of creating a non-profit where...once a week we'd go on a trip within San Diego, I mean some of the kids had never been to the beach, go to Coronado, go on a hike. Once a month taking the kids to a place outside of San Diego, maybe L.A. or the desert, and once a year actually taking them out of the state or out of the country.

Cindy was haunted by Julio's idea.

> I was freaking out. This is the best idea I've ever heard.... I literally wanted to quit my job and start this program for these kids. And that was his idea. It came from his idea. So...if I could do anything and money weren't an issue, I would focus each of our projects on a community-based idea and have [my students] create them because they've been through the experiences. And then give them the right people, resources, whatever it took, to make the goal actually come off the ground. We would change their communities completely. And what would it do for them to become leaders, running

organizations rather than running the streets? That would be my dream come true.

Until those dreams are realized, the teachers working on PBL at Momentum Learning continue to give students the opportunity to do meaningful work under the most challenging of circumstances. Nasim, Cindy's student whose spoken word performance catalyzed project-based learning across Momentum's network, is now 17 and recently graduated from high school. A year before his graduation, at a San Diego County Board of Education meeting, Nasim shared his reflections about the impact of TIP on the juvenile court and community schools.

> Two key words that popped out to me was passionate and commitment. I think that over the years of me coming to JCCS, over the past three, almost four, years, passion and commitment has been lacked. But now I think of it today, and personally I see a big improvement. Not 100%, but you guys are striving for it.... I'm glad to see that the change is starting. It gives me hope for my generation to come, and my kids, I might put them in JCCS to begin with! If it wasn't for the exhibitions, I think change would not have started. I think a lot of things would have stayed the same. I think I would not have been here in this chair. The exhibition made me feel engaged. It had me craving my learning. It's definitely inspired me to want to come to school...What I like about the whole TIP program is that it's not just you do this assignment and you get the answer, you get the results, you get your A, you get your B, or whatever. I feel like the teacher too...I'm educating myself for the better of myself.

Like Matt, Nasim sees the wisdom of Momentum's investment in growing the capacity of both students and adults. "Expanding the learning for teachers? That made me smile. 'Cause it's not just us students who need to expand. Everybody's always growing."

References and Resources

Youth Law Center, "Educational Injustice: Barriers to Achievement and Higher Education for Youth in California Juvenile Court Schools," San Francisco, 2016, http://www.ylc.org/wp/wp-content/uploads/ EDUCATIONAL%20INJUSTICE.pdf.

About the Authors

Mike Amarillas
Mike Amarillas studied physics at Stanford University but couldn't handle summer cooped up in a laboratory. He took a job as a YMCA camp counselor and became convinced his future was in teaching. After receiving his B.S. in physics, Mike entered the Stanford Teacher Education Program to obtain a teaching credential and M.Ed. He spent the next six years teaching physics in the Silicon Valley, working with English learners. In 2015, he returned to his native San Diego and joined the team at High Tech High North County. Mike currently teaches engineering and coordinates his school's makerspace.

Daisy Sharrock
Daisy Sharrock leads the Mathematical Agency Improvement Community (MAIC), a network of 18 southern California schools working to abolish the phrase "I am not a math person." The network of teachers and administrators convened by the Center for Research on Equity and Innovation at the High Tech High Graduate School of Education, use improvement science tools and methodologies to identify, test, and scale classroom practices that increase students' mathematical agency and success. Daisy also facilitates adult learning in the High Tech High Graduate School of Education Master's program, conducts improvement science professional development across the High Tech High K-12 schools, and assists in the development and convening of an improvement network drawn from California schools, districts and CMOs within the Deeper Learning network to tackle the persistent problem of college, career and civic readiness for all students. Daisy has a degree in biochemistry from the University of British Columbia, a master's in education from the High Tech High Graduate School of Education and is currently enrolled in a doctoral program through the University of California, San Diego.

Kali Frederick

Kali Frederick is an eighth grade humanities teacher at High Tech Middle Chula Vista. Since joining the staff at High Tech High she has found inspiration in interdisciplinary (or anti-disciplinary) teaching partnerships and co-creating projects with students, colleagues, and community groups. Kali earned her Associated Arts degree from NYU, Bachelor's Degree from the University of MN, Masters in the Science of Teaching from Pace University and her Master of Education in teacher leadership from the High Tech High Graduate School of Education.

Stephanie Lytle

Stephanie Lytle is a twelfth grade English teacher at High Tech High International. She earned her Bachelor of Arts degree in English from the University of California at Berkeley, her teaching credential from San Jose State University, and her M.Ed. in Teacher Leadership with the High Tech High Graduate School of Education. She works to integrate ever-evolving technology into classroom projects and strives to enable students to build an increased understanding of cultural foundations while examining art, music, and story.

Lillian Hsu

Lillian Hsu is the Founding Principal of Latitude High 37.8 in Oakland, California. Previously, she served as the Director of High Tech High Chula Vista. Lillian has worked in a variety of educational settings, including EdWeek's Teacher Magazine, the television program Sesame Street, and the Metropolitan Museum of Art. Lillian earned her bachelor of arts in psychology from Yale University, her master of arts in teaching from Brown University, and her master of education in school leadership from the High Tech High Graduate School of Education.

About the Editors

Stephen F. Hamilton
Stephen F. Hamilton is Professor Emeritus of Human Development at Cornell University, where he was also Associate Director of the Bronfenbrenner Center for Translational Research and Associate Provost for Outreach. He served as Dean of the High Tech High Graduate School of Education. He was educated at Swarthmore College and the Harvard Graduate School of Education and taught for three years at Phelps Vocational High School in Washington, DC. His research interests are in adolescent development and education, especially work-based learning, service-learning, and mentoring. As a Fulbright Senior Research Fellow, he studied Germany's apprenticeship system. He has also engaged in action research with colleagues in four Latin American youth programs.

Randy Scherer
Randy Scherer directs the California Career Pathways PBL Leadership Academy, a professional development program developed in conjunction with the California Department of Education Career Pathways Trust. Prior to that, Randy taught humanities at High Tech High Media Arts for ten years, where we was a founding member of the faculty. Randy was a founding member and editor of *UnBoxed: A Journal of Adult Learning in Schools*. He now develops and facilitates workshops on project-based learning and school reform for educators and policy makers in the US and abroad. Randy received his B.A. in Political Science and English from Binghamton University, his teaching credential from the University of San Diego and his M.Ed. in Teacher Leadership from the High Tech High Graduate School of Education.

Acknowledgements

Creating *Inspiration, Not Replication: How Teachers Are Leading School Change From the Inside* and the accompanying volume *Hands and Minds: A Guide to Project-Based Learning for Teachers by Teachers*, would not have been possible without the support of a diverse community of passionate educators, students, and professionals across the state of California, the United States, and beyond.

We sincerely appreciate the dedicated professionals at the California Career Pathways Trust and the California Department of Education. Thank you to Abby Medina Lewis, Joe Radding, Karen Shores, Russ Weikle, and Donna Wyatt, whose support was essential to this work.

We express our gratitude to Larry Rosenstock and Rob Riordan, High Tech High co-founders, who provided seemingly endless and invaluable insight into the pursuit of equity in education; Brent Spirnak, whose videography and photography was vital to the research that went into this project, and can be found online at hightechhigh.org; Enrique Lugo, for his creative vision and providing the cover design; Carmen Ramirez for supporting this project at every step; Felicia Hamway, Justine Aldridge, Kristy Renken, Kay McElrath, and Jenny Salkeld for ensuring sound business practices; and to Stephen Hamilton and Tom Fehrenbacher for editing these publications.

We are indebted to the teams of HTH Team Mentors who shared their endless passion and expertise for this work and who supported the PBL Leadership Academy teams: Emily Carter, Tina Chavez, Alicia Crump, Georgia Figueroa, Andrew Gloag, Kelly Jacob, Julia Jacobson, Mari Jones, Shani Leader, Charlie Linnik, Don MacKay, Jeremy Manger, Maggie Miller, Rachel Nichols, Mark Poole, Zoe Randall, John Santos, Mele Sato, Mackenzie

Schultz, David Smith, and Janna Steffan.

We could not have completed this without the broader community of HTH educators at all schools and all grade levels. Many thanks to Mark Aguirre, Sarah Barnes, Cate Challen, Tina Chavez, Corey Clark, Ben Daley, Janie Griswold, Jessica Hoffman, Pat Holder, Jamelle Jones, Chris Olivas, Kaleb Rashad, Juli Ruff, Jesse Wade-Robinson, Kelly Wilson, and Jade White.

Thank you to the guest faculty who lent their time, expertise, and boundless energy towards the PBL Leadership Academy: Ron Berger, Ashanti Branch, Victor Diaz, Albert Yu Min Lin, Emily Pilloton, Katie Rast, Tony Simmons, Adria Steinberg, Elliot Washor, and Yong Zhao.

We could not have produced these volumes without the educators who graciously opened their schools, classrooms, and hearts to us: the students from Windsor High School who shared their insider view of project-based learning and provided valuable advice on project design with Sonoma teachers during the C3 Project Based Learning Institute—and to Chuck Wade, Jessica Progulske, and the Sonoma County Office of Education team that made it possible; Dawn Miller of the Lindsay Community School, San Diego, for providing an exemplary model of how to provide students with rich social experiences; Erica Palicki, Samantha Howerton, and Dorothy Corona from S.O.A.R. Academy East Mesa; Matt Simon and the entire Momentum Learning team across San Diego County; Adam Brown from the Dublin School in Dublin, CA, for contributing effective strategies for employing academic reflection in engineering classes; Kate Casale of the Alameda County Office of Education; Lorilee Niessen of the Capital Region Academies for the Next Economy (CRANE), who shared her expertise, time, and resources, and took our writers from school to school to see first-hand about how they are transforming the teacher and student experience via PBL; The entire team at Central Coast New Tech High School, and Jennifer Isbell and Jennifer Stillittano for taking time for extensive interviews and providing valuable resources; the engineering department from Dublin High School in the Bay Area; "The PBL Team" at Anderson Valley Junior Senior High School; Joshua Dresser at Chicago Tech Academy; and Tammie Halloway at Napa County Office of Education.

We extend a deep thank you to the many fantastic, creative, and tireless educators who we worked with from the following schools, districts, and counties: Academy of the Canyons Middle College High School; Alameda County Office Of Education; Anderson Valley Unified School District; Antelope Valley Community College; Assurance Learning Academy; Capital Region Academies for the Next Economy (CRANE); Centinela Valley Union High School District; Contra Costa County Office of Education; Coronado Unified School District; Delhi Unified School District; Diego Valley Charter School; Downey Unified School District; Fresno Unified School District; Glendale Unified School District; Grossmont High School; Inglewood Unified School District; John Muir Charter Schools; Konocti Unified School District; Liberty Ranch High School; Livermore Valley Joint Unified School District; Los Angeles Unified School District; Mariposa County Unified School District; Momentum Learning schools including the Lindsay School, North County Community Schools, South County Community Schools, the Monarch School, S.O.A.R. Academy East Mesa; Montebello Unified School District; Napa County Office of Education; Northern Humboldt Union High School District; Orange County Department of Education; Oxnard Union High School District; Placentia–Yorba Linda School District; Paramount Career Prep Academy; San Luis Obispo Community College

District; San Luis Obispo County Office of Education; Santa Clarita Community College School District; Shasta College; Solano County Office of Education; Sonoma County Office of Education; Sutter County Office of Education; Tulare County Office of Education; Ventura County Office of Education; Victor Valley College; Visalia Unified School District; W.E.B. DuBois Public Charter School; West Placer Unified School District; West Valley College; Yosemite Community College District.

We are thankful for the support of the following educational organizations: Big Picture Learning, EL Learning, the National Writing Project, New Tech Network for supporting this work.

We are forever grateful to all of our families for supporting this work.

Made in the USA
San Bernardino, CA
28 June 2017